HAT
YOGA

CW01307742

Contact: oneofakindbooks@bhagwan.se

Bhagwan
One of a Kind Books

HATHA
YOGA

ISBN 9798546484668

***

The

HATHA YOGA PRADIPIKA

Introduced by Shreyananda Natha

Contact: oneofakindbooks@bhagwan.se

Publisher: ***BHAGWAN 2021***

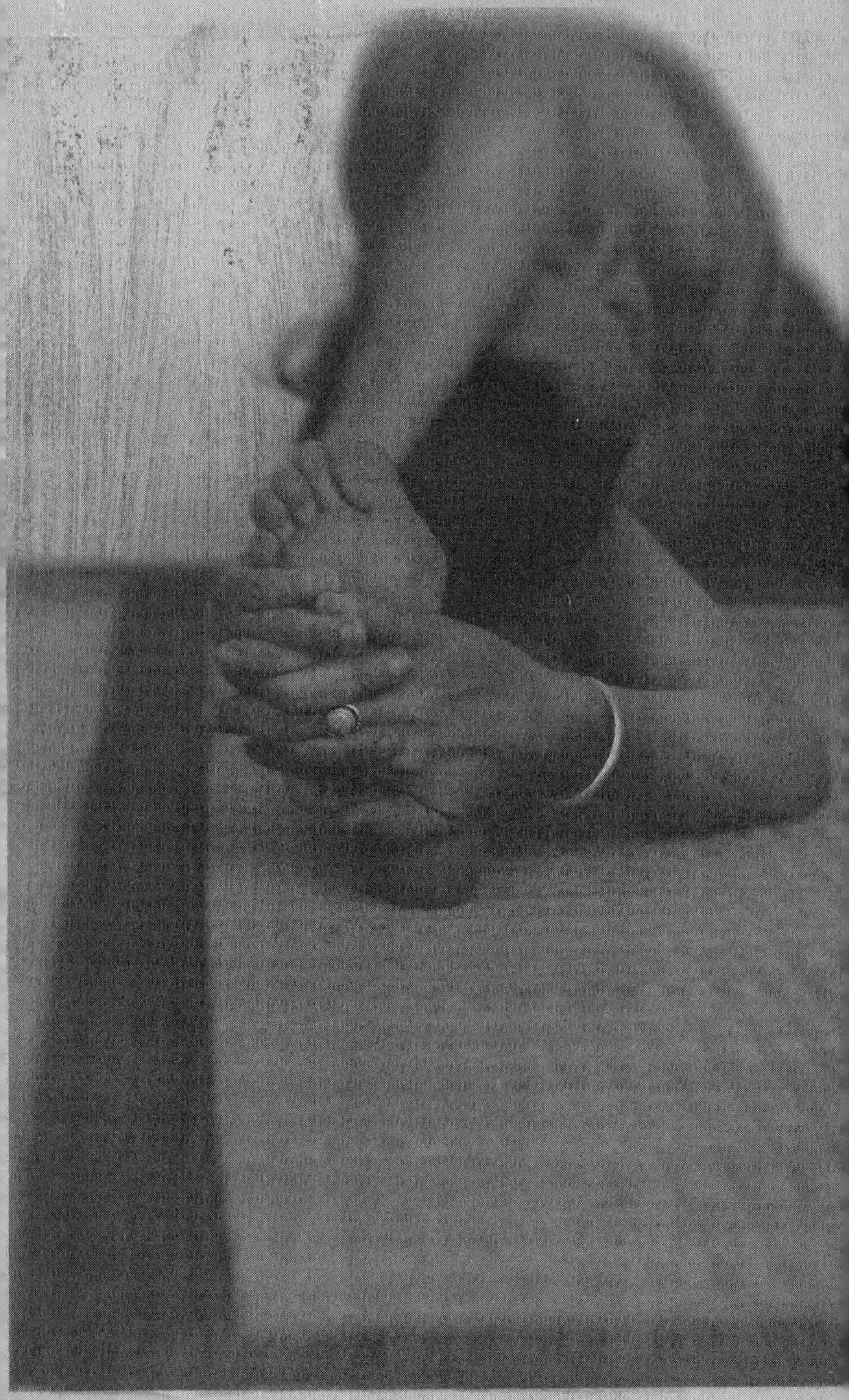

ॐ

"As one opens the door with a key, so the yogi should open the gate to liberation with the kundalini.

The great goddess sleeps, closing with her mouth, the opening through which one can ascend to the Brahmarandhra…
to that place where there is neither pain nor suffering.

The kundalini sleeps above the kanda…
she gives liberation to the yogi and bondage to the fool.

He who knows kundalini, knows yoga.

The kundalini, it is said, is coiled like a serpent.
He who can induce her to move is liberated."

Hatha Yoga Pradipika v. 105-111.

Index

Introduction

Hatha Yoga Pradipika.

Is the No.1 most read book about yoga besides Patanjalis Yogasutras. The Hatha Yoga Pradipika, along with the Gheranda-Samhita (1650), is one of the most detailed manuals describing the techniques of Hatha Yoga. The book is the hatha yoga text that has historically been studied within yoga teacher training programmes, alongside texts on classical yoga such as Patanjali's Yoga Sutras.

The HYP is a medieval yoga text, dating from about the 15th or 16th century, and is as much about Tantra as about Yoga. It was compiled by Swātmārama. It´s name means "special (pra) light (dipika) on forceful (hatha) yoga". It is much later in date than the Yoga Sutras, and provides details of Hatha Yoga techniques which the Yoga Sutras don't touch on. But there are also occasional sutras which touch on familiar concerns (for example, compare HYP 4.23 with YS 1.2). It is just about yoga practice, as contrasted with the Bhagavad Gītā, which is about how to live in the everyday world.

The word "hatha" requires a little comment. The concept

is that we live in an energy field; energy is behind all action. The energy field that we live in normally extends 4 fingers-breadth beyond the body, and it is possible also in a healthy person to achieve a situation in which the energy is concentrated inside the body. In an unhealthy person the energy dissipates further. There are blockages in an unhealthy person that makes it impossible to concentrate one's energy properly, and techniques such as nadi śodhana are used to open the channels and improve the flow of energy.

There is in fact a whole complex of energy channels or nāḍī within the body, of which there are 11 primary nadi, coming from a central hub (kanda) located in the lower abdomen, and branching out into many others (traditionally, 72,000).

There are 10 nadi associated with perception and action:

eyes (sight)

tongue (speech)

ears (hearing)

fingers & thumbs (grasping)

tongue (taste)

big toes (locomotion)

skin (feeling)

bladder & anus (excretion)

nostrils (smell)

sex organs (generation)

If the quality of the nadi is poor, the quality of perception and action is also poor.

There is one more nadi, the susumna, which instead of flowing out, flows in, linking us to the inner world. It runs from the kanda to the base of the spine then to the top of the head. There are two processes in energy, ha and tha, which flow through the pingala and ida channels (or nādī) respectively, and then unite to flow into susumna. Usually it is not possible for energy to flow into susumna because of a blockage at the base of the spine. The practice of Hatha Yoga tries to create a state of breakthrough allowing energy to flow into susumna, bringing with it a stable state of mind. The Hatha Yoga Pradipika teaches techniques that allow this state to be achieved.

The difference between the Hatha Yoga of the Hatha Yoga Pradipika and the Raja Yoga of the Yoga Sutras is that Hatha Yoga uses prana as a primary working tool, whereas Raja Yoga uses the mind as its primary working tool. These days very few people are able to practice Hatha Yoga sufficiently strongly for it to work properly.

The key ideas in the text are:

Chapter 1 – āsana: used to stimulate energy (prana);
Chapter 2 – prāṇāyāma: used to contain/condense energy;
Chapter 3 – mudrā: used to direct energy;
Chapter 4 – dhyāna: used to integrate and merge energy.

Chapter Summaries:

CHAPTER 1: Asanas.
1-11 Introduction.
Hatha yoga "shines forth as a stairway to raja yoga" (1); is "the greatest secret of the yogis who wish to attain perfection".
12-16 Conditions for practice.
The "hermitage" described (12-14); obstacles and supports (15-16). The ten yama and ten niyama in sutras 16ii and 16iii are apparently later additions to the text; hatha yoga does not in fact place much emphasis on them.

17-56 Āsana.

The role of āsana is to develop steadiness of body and mind, flexibility of the limbs; sequence for practice is āsana → prānāyāma → mudrā → meditation (56).

57-63 Diet and Restrictions.

Mitāhāra – appropriate food (57, 62-63); food to avoid (58-59); other things to avoid (60-61).

64-67 Conclusion.

Importance of practical application emphasised (64-66); hatha yoga leads to Raja Yoga (67).

CHAPTER 2: Prāṇāyāmas.

1-3 Breath and mind.

First make the body steady, then bring steadiness to prāna (1); when prāna moves, citta moves (2).

4-5 Nādī and malā.

Nadīs must be purified so that prāna can flow.

6-20 Practice guidelines.

Practice daily (6); nadi śodhana (7-12); milk and ghee important foods (14); negative effects of inappropriate practice (15-17); indications of purification (18-20).

21-36 The Śat Karma (cleansing techniques).

These should be practised only by persons with kapha imbalance (21).

37-74 Prānāyāma.

Some teachers say prānāyāma alone is enough to cleanse the system (37); prānāyāma purifies the nādīs and chakras, and opens the door to suśumna (41); manonmani – mind devoid of thought (42); eight types of kumbhaka (43-70); three processes of prānāyāma (71-74); two processes of kumbhaka (72-74).

75-77 Kundalini and Raja Yoga.

By practising kumbhaka, kundalini is aroused and suśumna is freed of obstacles (75); both hatha and raja yoga are essential for perfection (samādhi) (76).

78 Eight signs of perfection.

lean body, bright face, strong voice, clear eyes, no disease, control of semen, active digestive fire, purification of nādis.

CHAPTER 3: Mudrās.

1-2 Kundalini.

Kundalini the support of all yoga practices.

3-5 Susumnā.

When kundalini awakens, susumnā becomes pathway of prāna (3); the "goddess sleeping at Brahma's door" can be aroused by performing mudrā.

6-103 Ten mudrās described.

10-18 maha mudra.

19-25 maha bandha.

26-29 maha vedha.

30-31 when to perform these three.

32-54 khechari mudra.

55-60 uddiyana bandha.

61-69 mula bandha.

70-73 jalandhara bandha.

74-77 comments on the three bandhas.

78-82 viparita karani.

83-91 vajroli mudra.

92-95 sahajoli mudra.

96-103 maroli mudra.

104-124 Kundalini.

Kundalini is coiled like a snake(108), 3½ times, at base of susumnā; you have to awaken the snake (111) [like getting rid of a snake in a tree by either hitting the tree with a stick or lighting a fire under it]; this moves kundalini so that it is drawn up into susumnā a little way (117), thus allowing prāna to enter susumnā (118). Best way to do this is to practise bhastrika with kumbhaka (122); other than arousing kundalini, the other way to purify the nadis including susumnā is regular practice of āsana, prānāyāma, mudrā and concentration (124).

125-127 Importance of mental attitude.

Prānāyāma should be practised with a focused mind.

128-130 Conclusion.

CHAPTER 4: Samādhi.

1-9 Samādhi.

Mind and ātman come together in samādhi.

10-29 Prāna.

When prāna flows in susumnā, the mind is blank (12);

as well as prāna, air and fire enter suśumnā (19); when mind is still, prāna is suspended, when prāna is suspended, mind is still (23); if they are controlled, moksa (liberation) is attained (25); this brings steadiness to the body (28).

30-34 Laya (dissolution)

Definition of laya (31).

35-37 Śambhavi mudra (eyebrow centre gazing).

38-47 Khecari.

48 Tūrya.

This "fourth state" is one in which the mind is quiescent.

49-53 Yoga Nidrā.

This is the state in which the conscious mind subsides but awareness remains. It's like a pot filled with space (50).

54-63 Samādhi.

64-102 Nāda.

The sound created by the union of Śiva and Śakti.

Four stages of yoga practice (69-77).

Raja yoga (78-79).

Modern research.

The Hatha Yoga Pradipika is the hatha yoga text that has historically been studied within yoga teacher training programmes, alongside texts on classical yoga such as Patanjali's Yoga Sutras. In the twenty-first century, research on the history of yoga has led to a more developed understanding of hatha yoga's origins.

James Mallinson has studied the origins of hatha yoga in classic yoga texts such as the Khecarīvidyā. He has identified eight works of early hatha yoga that may have contributed to its official formation in the Hatha Yoga Pradipika. This has stimulated further research into understanding the formation of hatha yoga.

Jason Birch has investigated the role of the Hatha Yoga Pradīpikā in popularizing an interpretation of the Sanskrit word hatha. The text drew from classic texts on different systems of yoga, and Svātmārāma grouped what he had found under the generic term "hatha yoga". Examining Buddhist tantric commentaries and earlier medieval yoga texts, Birch found that the adverbial uses of the word suggested that it meant "force", rather than "the metaphysical explanation proposed in the 14th century Yogabīja of uniting the sun (ha) and moon (tha.

The Hatha Yoga Pradipika is also an ocean of secret/hidden knowledge.

Seeker. Listen to this vers:

"As one opens the door with a key, so the yogi should open the gate to liberation with the kundalini.

The great goddess sleeps, closing with her mouth,
the opening through which one can ascend to the Brahmarandhra...
to that place where there is neither pain nor suffering.

The kundalini sleeps above the kanda...
she gives liberation to the yogi and bondage to the fool.

He who knows kundalini, knows yoga.

The kundalini, it is said, is coiled like a serpent.
He who can induce her to move is liberated."

Hatha Yoga Pradipika v. 105-111.

Om Sri Durgayai Namah

Remebering we are one. Be always united with the force of the universe. She will take care about you but not for free. Remember this.

Yogi Shreyananda Natha

Chapter 1

ASANAS

Prathamopadeśah

1.) śrī-ādi-nāthāya namo|astu tasmai yeno-padiṣhṭā haṭha-yogha-vidyā I vibhrājate pronnata-rāja-yogham āroḍhumichchorad-hirohiṇīva

Salutations to Shiva, who taught the science of Hatha Yoga.
It is the aspirant's stairway to the heights of Raja Yoga.

2.) praṇamya śrī-ghuruṃ nāthaṃ svātmārā-meṇa yoghinā I kevalaṃ rāja-yoghāya haṭha-vidyopadiśyate

Yogi Svatmarama, after saluting the Lord and guru, explains the science of Hatha for one reason – Raja Yoga.

3.) bhrāntyā bahumata-dhvānte rāja-yogha-majānatām I haṭha-pradīpikāṃ dhatte svāt-mārāmaḥ kṛpākaraḥ

For those ignorant of Raja Yoga, wandering in the darkness of too many opinions, compassionate Svatmarama gives the light of Hatha.

4.) haṭha-vidyāṃ hi matsyendra-ghorakṣhā-dyā vijānate I svātmārāmo|athavā yoghī jānīte tat-prasādataḥ

Matsyendra, Goraksha, and others know well the science of Hatha. By their grace, Yogi Svatmarama also knows it.

The following Siddhas (masters) are said to have existed in former times. Guru-shishya means "succession from Guru to disciple". Paramparā literally means an uninterrupted row or series, order, succession, continuation, mediation, tradition.

5.) śrī-ādinātha-matsyendra-śāvarānan-da-bhairavāḥ I chaurangghī-mīna-gho-rakṣha-virūpākṣha-bileśayāḥ

Sri Âdinâtha (Śiva), Matsyendra, Nâtha, Sâbar, Anand, Bhairava, Chaurangi, Mîna nâtha, Goraksanâtha, Virupâksa, Bileśaya.

6.) manthāno bhairavo yoghī siddhirbudd-haścha kanthaḍiḥ I koraṃṭakaḥ surānandaḥ siddhapādaścha charpaṭiḥ

Manthâna, Bhairava, Siddhi Buddha, Kanthadi, Karantaka, Surânanda, Siddhipâda, Charapati.

7.) kānerī pūjyapādaścha nitya-nātho nirañjanaḥ I kapālī bindunāthaścha kākachaṇḍīśvarāhvayaḥ

Kânerî, Pûjyapâda, Nityanâtha, Nirañjana, Kapâli, Vindunâtha, Kâka Chandîśwara.

8.) allāmaḥ prabhudevaścha ghoḍā cholī cha ṭiṃṭiṇiḥ I bhānukī nāradevaścha khaṇḍaḥ kāpālikastathā

Allâma, Prabhudeva, Ghodâ, Cholî, Tintini, Bhânukî Nârdeva, Khanda Kâpâlika, etc.

9.) ityādayo mahāsiddhā haṭha-yogha-prabhāvataḥ I khaṇḍayitvā kāla-daṇḍaṃ brahmāṇḍe vicharanti te

These Mahâsiddhas (great masters), having conquered death through the power of Hatha Yoga, roam the universe.

10.) aśeṣha-tāpa-taptānāṃ samāśraya-maṭho haṭhaḥ I aśeṣha-yogha-yuktānāmādhāra-ka-maṭho haṭhaḥ

Hatha is the sanctuary for those suffering every type of pain.

It is the foundation for those practicing every type of Yoga.

11.) haṭha-vidyā paraṃ ghopyā yoghinā siddhimichchatā I bhavedvīryavatī ghuptā nirvīryā tu prakāśitā

A Yogî desirous of success should keep the knowledge of Hatha Yoga secret; for it becomes potent by concealing, and impotent by exposing.

12.) surājye dhārmike deśe subhikṣhe nirupadrave I dhanuḥ pramāṇa-paryantaṃ śilāghni-jala-varjite I ekānte maṭhikā-madhye sthātavyaṃ haṭha-yoghinā

The Yogî should practise Hatha Yoga in a small room, situated in a solitary place, being 4 cubits square, and free from stones, fire, water, disturbances of all kinds, and in a country where justice is properly administered, where good people live, and food can be obtained easily and plentifully.

13.) alpa-dvāramarandhra-gharta-vivaraṃ nātyuchcha-nīchāyataṃ samyagh-gho-maya-sāndra-liptamamalaṃ niḥśesa-jantūjjhi-tam I bāhye maṇḍapa-vedi-kūpa-ruchiraṃ

prākāra-saṃveṣhṭitaṃ proktaṃ yogha-maṭhasya lakṣhaṇamidaṃ siddhair-haṭhābhyāsibhiḥ

The room should have a small door, be free from holes, hollows, neither too high nor too low, well plastered with cow-dung and free from dirt, filth and insects. On its outside there should be bowers, raised platform (chabootrâ), a well, and a compound. These characteristics of a room for Hatha Yogîs have been described by adepts in the practice of Hatha.

14.) aevaṃ vidhe maṭhe sthitvā sarva-chintā-vivarjitaḥ I ghurūpadiṣhṭa-mārghena yoghameva samabhyaset

Having seated in such a room and free from all anxieties, he should practise Yoga, as instructed by his Guru.

15.) atyāhāraḥ prayāsaścha prajalpo niyamāghrahaḥ I jana-sangghaścha laulyaṃ cha ṣhaḍbhiryogho vinaśyati

Yoga perishes by these six: overeating, overexertion, talking too much, performing needless austerities, social-izing, and restlessness.

16.) utsāhātsāhasāddhairyāttattva-jñānāścha niśchayāt I jana-sanggha-parityāg-hātṣhaḍbhiryoghaḥ prasiddhyati

Yoga succeeds by these six: enthusiasm, openness, courage, knowledge of the truth, determination, and solitude.

17.) atha yama-niyamāḥ ahiṃsā satyamasteyaṃ brahmacharyaṃ kṣhamā dhṛtiḥ I dayārjavaṃ mitāhāraḥ śauchaṃ chaiva yamā daśa

The ten rules of conduct are: ahimsâ (non-injuring), truth, non-stealing, continence, forgiveness, endurance, compassion, meekness, sparing diet and cleanliness.

18.) tapaḥ santoṣha āstikyaṃ dānamīśvara-pūjanam I siddhānta-vākya-śravaṇaṃ hrīmatī cha tapo hutam I niyamā daśa samproktā yogha-śāstra-viśāradaiḥ

The ten niyamas mentioned by those proficient in the knowledge of yoga are: Tapa, patience, belief in God, charity, adoration of God, hearing discourses on the principles of religion, shame, intellect, Tapa and Yajña.

19.) atha āsanam haṭhasya prathamāngghatvādāsanaṃ pūrvamuchyate I kuryāttadāsanaṃ sthairyamāroghyaṃ chānggha-lāghavam

Being the first accessory of Hatha Yoga, âsana is described first. It should be practised for gaining steady posture, health and lightness of body.

20.) vaśiṣhṭhādyaiścha munibhirmatsyendrādyaiścha yoghibhiḥ I angghīkṝtānyāsanāni kathyante kānichinmayā

I am going to describe certain âsanas which have been adopted by Munîs like Vasistha and Yogîs like Matsyendra.

21.) jānūrvorantare samyakkṝtvā pāda-tale ubhe I ṝju-kāyaḥ samāsīnaḥ svastikaṃ tatprachakṣhate

Swastika-âsana.

Having kept both the hands under both the thighs, with the body straight, when one sits calmly in this posture, it is called Swastika.

22.) savye dakṣhiṇa-ghulkaṃ tu pṝṣhṭhapārśve niyojayet I dakṣhiṇe|api tathā savyaṃ ghomukhaṃ ghomukhākṝtiḥ

Gomukha-âsana.

Placing the right ankle on the left side and the left ankle on the right side, makes Gomukha-âsana, having the appearance of a cow.

23.) ekaṃ pādaṃ tathaikasminvinyaseduruṇi sthiram I itarasmiṃstathā choruṃ vīrāsana-mitīritam

Vîrâsana.

One foot is to be placed on the thigh of the opposite side; and so also the other foot on the opposite thigh. This is called Vîrâsana.

24.) ghudaṃ nirudhya ghulphābhyāṃ vyut-krameṇa samāhitaḥ I kūrmāsanaṃ bhavede-taditi yogha-vido viduḥ

Kurmâsana.

Placing the right ankle on the left side of anus, and the left ankle on the right side of it, makes what the Yogîs call Kûrma-âsana.

25.) padmāsanaṃ tu saṃsthāpya jānūrvoran-tare karau I niveśya bhūmau saṃsthāpya vyomasthaṃ kukkuṭāsanam

Kukkuta-âsana.

Taking the posture of Padma-âsana and carrying the hands under the thighs, when the Yogî raises himself above the ground, with his palms resting on the ground, it becomes Kukkuta-âsana.

26.) kukkuṭāsana-bandha-stho dorbhyāṃ sambadya kandharām I bhavedkūrmavadut-tāna etaduttāna-kūrmakam

Uttâna Kûrma-âsana.

Having assumed Kukkuta-âsana, when one grasps his neck by crossing his hands behind his head, and lies in this posture with his back touching the ground, it becomes Uttâna Kûrma-âsana, from its appearance like that of a tortoise.

27.) pādāngghuṣhṭhau tu pāṇibhyāṃ ghṝhītvā śravaṇāvadhi I dhanurākarṣhaṇaṃ kuryādd-hanur-āsanamuchyate

Dhanura-âsana.

Having caught the toes of the feet with both the hands and carried them to the ears by drawing the body like a bow, it becomes Dhanura âsana.

28+29.) vāmoru-mūlārpita-dakṣha-pādaṃ jānorbahirveṣhṭita-vāma-pādam I praghṝhya tiṣhṭhetparivartitāngghaḥ śrī-matysanāthodi-tamāsanaṃ syāt

matsyendra-pīṭhaṃ jaṭhara-pradīptiṃ prachaṇḍa-rughmaṇḍala-khaṇḍanāstram I abhyāsataḥ kuṇḍalinī-prabodhaṃ chandra-st-hiratvaṃ cha dadāti puṃsām

Matsyendrâsana.

Having placed the right foot at the root of the left thigh, let the toe be grasped with the right hand passing over the back, and having placed the left foot on the right thigh at its root, let it be grasped with the left hand passing behind the back. This is the âsana, as explained by Śri Matsyanâtha.

It increases appetite and is an instrument for destroying the group of the most deadly diseases. Its practice awakens the Kundalinî, stops the nectar shedding from the moon in people.

30.) prasārya pādau bhuvi daṇḍa-rūpau dor-bhyāṃ padāghra-dvitayaṃ ghṝhītvā I jānūpa-rinyasta-lalāṭa-deśo vasedidaṃ paśchimatā-namāhuḥ

Paśchima Tâna.

Having stretched the feet on the ground, like a stick, and having grasped the toes of both the feet with both the hands, when one sits with his forehead resting on the thighs, it is called Paśchima Tâna.

31.) iti paśchimatānamāsanāghryaṃ pavanaṃ paśchima-vāhinaṃ karoti I udayaṃ jaṭharā-nalasya kuryād udare kārśyamaroghatāṃ cha puṃsām

This Paśchima Tâna carries the air from the front to the back part of the body (i.e., to the sushumna). It kindles gastric fire, reduces obesity and cures all diseases of men.

32.) dharāmavaṣhṭabhya kara-dvayena tat-kūrpara-sthāpita-nābhi-pārśvaḥ I uchchā-sano daṇḍavadutthitaḥ khe māyūrametatpra-vadanti pīṭham

Mayûra-âsana.

Place the palms of both the hands on the ground, and place the navel on both the elbows and balancing thus, the body should be stretched backward like a stick. This is called Mayûra-âsana.

33.) harati sakala-roghānāśu ghulmodarādīn abhibhavati cha doṣhānāsanaṃ śrī-mayūram I bahu kadaśana-bhuktaṃ bhasma kuryādaśeṣhaṃ janayati jaṭharāghniṃ jārayet-kāla-kūṭam

This Âsana soon destroys all diseases, and removes abdominal disorders, and also those arising from irregularities of phlegm, bile and wind, digests unwholesome food taken in excess, increases appetite and destroys the most deadly poison.

34.) uttānaṃ śabavadbhūmau śayanaṃ tachchavāsanam I śavāsanaṃ śrānti-haraṃ chitta-viśrānti-kārakam

Śava-âsana.

Lying down on the ground, like a corpse, is called Śava-âsana. It removes fatigue and gives rest to the mind.

35.) chaturaśītyāsanāni śivena kathitāni cha I tebhyaśchatuṣhkamādāya sārabhūtaṃ bravīmyaham

Śiva taught 84 âsanas. Of these the first four being essential ones, I am going to explain them here.

36.) siddhaṃ padmaṃ tathā siṃhaṃ bhadraṃ veti chatuṣhṭayam I śreṣhṭhaṃ tatrāpi cha sukhe tiṣhṭhetsiddhāsane sadā

These four are: The Siddha, Padma, Sinha and Bhadra. Even of these, the Siddha-âsana, being very comfortable, one should always practise it.

37.) atha siddhāsanam

yoni-sthānakamangghri-mūla-ghaṭitaṃ kṛtvā dṛḍhaṃ vinyaset meṇḍhre pādamathaikame-va hṛdaye kṛtvā hanuṃ susthiram I sthāṇuḥ saṃyamitendriyo|achala-dṛśā paśyedbh-ruvorantaraṃ hyetanmokṣha-kapāṭa-bhe-da-janakaṃ siddhāsanaṃ prochyate

The Siddhâsana.

Press firmly the heel of the left foot against the perineum, and the right heel above the male organ. With the chin pressing on the chest, one should sit calmly, having restrained the senses, and gaze steadily the space between the eyebrows. This is called the Siddha Âsana, the opener of the door of salvation.

38.) meṇḍhrādupari vinyasya savyaṃ ghulphaṃ tathopari I ghulphāntaraṃ cha nikṣhipya siddhāsanamidaṃ bhavet

This Siddhâsana is performed also by placing the left heel on Medhra (above the male organ), and then placing the right one on it.

39.) etatsiddhāsanaṃ prāhuranye vajrāsanaṃ viduḥ I muktāsanaṃ vadantyeke prāhurghuptāsanaṃ pare

Some call this Siddhâsana, some Vajrâsana. Others call it Mukta Âsana or Gupta Âsana.

40.) syameṣhviva mitāhāramahiṃsā niyameṣhviva I mukhyaṃ sarvāsaneṣhvekaṃ siddhāḥ siddhāsanaṃ viduḥ

Just as sparing food is among Yamas, and Ahimsâ among the Niyamas, so is Siddhâsana called by adepts the chief of all the âsanas.

41.) chaturaśīti-pītheshu siddhameva sadābhyaset I dvāsaptati-sahasrānām nādīnām mala-śodhanam

Out of the 84 Âsanas Siddhâsana should always be practised, because it cleanses the impurities of 72,000 nâdîs.

42.) ātma-dhyāyī mitāhārī yāvaddvādaśa-vatsaram I sadā siddhāsanābhyāsādyoghī nishpattimāpnuyāt

By contemplating on oneself, by eating sparingly, and by practising Siddhâsana for 12 years, the Yogî obtains success.

43.) kimanyairbahubhiḥ pīṭhaiḥ siddhe siddhāsane sati I prāṇānile sāvadhāne baddhe kevala-kumbhake I utpadyate nirāyāsātsvayamevonmanī kalā

Other postures are of no use, when success has been achieved in Siddhâsana, and Prâna Vâyû becomes calm and restrained by Kevala Kumbhaka.

44.) tathaikāsminneva drdhe siddhe siddhāsane sati I bandha-trayamanāyāsātsvayamevopajāyate

Success in one Siddhâsana alone becoming firmly established, one gets Unmanî at once, and the three bonds (Bandhas) are accomplished of themselves.

45.) nāsanaṃ siddha-sadṝśaṃ na kumbhaḥ kevalopamaḥ I na khecharī-samā mudrā na nāda-sadṝśo layaḥ

There is no Âsana like the Siddhâsana and no Kumbhaka like the Kevala. There is no mudrâ like the Khechari and no laya like the Nâda (Anâhata Nâda.)

46.) atha padmāsanam
vāmorūpari dakṣhiṇaṃ cha charaṇaṃ saṃsthāpya vāmaṃ tathā dakṣhorūpari paśchimena vidhinā dhṛtvā karābhyāṃ dṛḍham I angghuṣhṭhau hṛdaye nidhāya chibukaṃnāsāghramālokayet etadvyādhi-vināśa-kāri yamināṃ padmāsanaṃ prochyate

The Padmâsana.

Place the right foot on the left thigh and the left foot on the right thigh, and grasp the toes with the hands crossed over the back. Press the chin against the chest and gaze on the tip of the nose. This is called the Padmâsana, the destroyer of the diseases of the Yamîs.

47.) uttānau charaṇau kṛtvā ūru-saṃsthau prayatnataḥ I ūru-madhye tathottānau pāṇī kṛtvā tato dṛśau

Place the feet on the thighs, with the soles upwards, and place the hands on the thighs, with the palms upwards.

48.) nāsāghre vinyasedrājad-anta-mūle tu jihvayā I uttambhya chibukaṃ vakṣhasyutthāpy pavanaṃ śanaiḥ

Gaze on the tip of the nose, keeping the tongue pressed against the root of the teeth of the upper jaw, and the chin against the chest, and raise the air up slowly, i.e., pull the apâna-vâyû gently upwards.

49.) idaṃ padmāsanaṃ proktaṃ sarva-vyādhi-vināśanam I durlabhaṃ yena kenāpi dhīmatā labhyate bhuvi

This is called the Padmâsana, the destroyer of all diseases. It is difficult of attainment by everybody, but can be learnt by intelligent people in this world.

50.) kṝtvā samputịtau karau dṝḍhataraṃ baddhvā tu padmamāsanaṃ ghāḍhaṃ vakṣhasi sannidhāya chibukaṃ dhyāyaṃścha tachchetasi I vāraṃ vāramapānamūrdhvamanilaṃ protsārayanpūritaṃ nyañchanprāṇamupaiti bodhamatulaṃ śakti-prabhāvānnaraḥ

Having kept both the hands together in the lap, performing the Padmâsana firmly, keeping the chin Fixed to the chest and contemplating on Him in the mind, by drawing the apâna-vâyû up (performing Mûla Bandha) and pushing down the air after inhaling it, joining thus the prâna and apâna in the navel, one gets the highest intelligence by awakening the śakti (kundalinî) thus.

NB.—When Apâna Vâyû is drawn gently up and after filling in the lungs with the air from outside, the prâna is forced down by and by so as to join both of them in the navel, they both enter then the Kundalinî and, reaching the Brahma randhra (the great hole), they make the mind calm. Then the mind can contemplate on the nature of the âtmana and can enjoy the highest bliss.

51.) padmāsane sthito yoghī nāḍī-dvāreṇa pūritam mārutaṃ dhārayedyastu sa mukto nātra saṃśayaḥ

The Yogî who, sitting with Padmâsana, can control breathing, there is no doubt, is free from bondage.

52.) atha siṃhāsanam
ghulphau cha vṝṣhaṇasyādhaḥ sīvantyāḥ pārśvayoḥ kṣhipet I dakṣhiṇe savya-ghulpham tu dakṣha- ghulphaṃ tu savyake

The Simhâsana.

Press the heels on both sides of the seam of Perineum, in such a way that the left heel touches the right side and the right heel touches the left side of it.

53.) hastau tu jānvoḥ saṃsthāpya svānggh-hulīḥ sam-prasārya cha I vyātta-vakto nirīkṣ-heta nāsāgh-raṃ susamāhitaḥ

Place the hands on the thighs, with stretched fingers, and keeping the mouth open and the mind collected, gaze on the tip of the nose.

54.) siṃhāsanaṃ bhavedetatpūjitaṃ yog-hi-pungghavaiḥ I bandha-tritaya-sandhānaṃ kurute chāsanottamam

This is Simhâsana, held sacred by the best of Yogîs. This excellent Âsana effects the completion of the three Band-has (The Mûlabandha, Kantha or Jâlandhar Bandha and Uddiyâna Bandha).

55+56.) atha bhadrāsanam
ghulphau cha vṝṣhaṇasyādhaḥ sīvantyāḥ pārśvayoḥ kṣhipte I savya-ghulphaṃ tathā savye dakṣha-ghulphaṃ tu dakṣhiṇe

pārśva-pādau cha pāṇibhyāṃ dṝḍhaṃ baddh-vā suniśchalam I bhadrāsanaṃ bhavedetats-

arva-vyādhi-vināśanam I ghorakṣhāsanami-tyāhuridaṃ vai siddha-yoghinaḥ

The Bhadrâsana.

Place the heels on either side of the seam of the Perineum, keeping the left heel on the left side and the right one on the right side, hold the feet firmly joined to one another with both the hands. This Bhadrâsana is the destroyer of all the diseases.

57.) evamāsana-bandheṣhu yoghīndro vighata-śramaḥ I abhyasennāḍikā-śuddhiṃ mudrādi-pavanī-kriyām

The expert Yogîs call this Gorakśa âsana. By sitting with this âsana, the Yogî gets rid of fatigue.

58.) āsanaṃ kumbhakaṃ chitraṃ mudrākhyaṃ karaṇaṃ tathā I atha nādānusandhānamabhyāsānukramo haṭhe

The Nâdis should be cleansed of their impurities by performing the mudrâs, etc. (which are the practices relating to the air). Âsanas, Kumbhakas and various curious mûdrâs.

59.) brahmachārī mitāhārī tyāghī yog-ha-parāyaṇaḥ I abdādūrdhvaṃ bhavedsidd-ho nātra kāryā vichāraṇā

By regular and close attention to Nâda (anâhata nâda) in Hatha Yoga, a Brahmachari, sparing in diet, unattached to objects of enjoyment, and devoted to Yoga, gains success, no doubt, within a year.

60.) susnighdha-madhurāhāraścha-turthāṃśa-vivarjitaḥ I bhujyate śi-va-samprītyai mitāhāraḥ sa uchyate

Abstemious feeding is that in which ¾ of hunger is satisfied with food, well cooked with ghee and sweets, and eaten with the offering of it to Śiva.

61.) kaṭvāmla-tīkṣhṇa-lavaṇoṣhṇa-harīta-śāka-sauvīra-taila-tila-sarṣhapa-madya-matsyān I ājādi-māṃsa-dadhi-takra-kulatthakola-piṇyāka-hingghu-laśunādyamapathyamāhuḥ

Foods injurious to a Yogî.

Bitter, sour, saltish, hot, green vegetables, fermented, oily, mixed with til seed, rape seed, intoxicating liquors, fish, meat, curds, chhaasa pulses, plums, oil-cake, asafoetida (hînga), garlic, onion, etc. should not be eaten.

62.) sbhojanamahitaṃ vidyātpuna-rasyoṣhṇī-kṛtaṃ rūkṣham I atilavaṇamam-la-yuktaṃ kadaśana-śākotkaṃ varjyam

Food heated again, dry, having too much salt, sour, minor grains, and vegetables that cause burning sensation, should not be eaten, Fire, women, travelling, etc., should be avoided.

63.) vahni-strī-pathi-sevānāmādau varja-namācharet

As said by Goraksa, one should keep aloof from the society of the evil-minded, fire, women, travelling, early morning bath, fasting, and all kinds of bodily exertion.

64.) tathā hi ghorakṣha-vachanam varjayed-durjana-prāntaṃ vahni-strī-pathi-sevanam I prātaḥ-snānopavāsādi kāya-kleśa-vidhiṃ tathā

Wheat, rice, barley, shâstik (a kind of rice), good corns, milk, ghee, sugar, butter, sugarcandy, honey, dried ginger, Parwal (a vegetable) the five vegetables, moong, pure water, these are very beneficial to those who practise Yoga.

65.) hodhūma-śāli-yava-ṣhāṣhṭika-śobhanān-naṃ kṣhīrājya-khaṇḍa-navanīta-sidd-hā-madhūni I śuṇṭhī-paṭola-kaphalādi-ka-pañcha-śākaṃ mudghādi-divyamudakaṃ cha yamīndra-pathyam

A Yogî should eat tonics (things giving strength), well sweetened, greasy (made with ghee), milk, butter, etc., which may increase humors of the body, according to his desire.

66.) puṣhṭaṃ sumadhuraṃ snighdhaṃ ghavy-aṃ dhātu-prapoṣhaṇam I manobhilaṣhitaṃ yoghyaṃ yoghī bhojanamācharet

Whether young, old or too old, sick or lean, one who discards laziness, gets success if he practises Yoga.

67.) yuvo vṝddho|ativṝddho vā vyādhito dur-balo|api vā I abhyāsātsiddhimāpnoti sar-va-yogheṣhvatandritaḥ

Success comes to him who is engaged in the practice. How can one get success without practice; for by merely reading books on Yoga, one can never get success.

68.) kriyā-yuktasya siddhiḥ syādakriyasya

kathaṃ bhavet I na śāstra-pāṭha-mātreṇa yogha-siddhiḥ prajāyate

Success cannot be attained by adopting a particular dress (Vesa). It cannot be gained by telling tales. Practice alone is the means to success. This is true, there is no doubt.

69+70.) na veṣha-dhāraṇaṃ siddheḥ kāraṇaṃ na cha tat-kathā I kriyaiva kāraṇaṃ siddheḥ satyametanna saṃśayaḥ

pīṭhāni kumbhakāśchitrā divyāni karaṇāni cha I sarvāṇyapi haṭhābhyāse rāja-yog-ha-phalāvadhi

Âsanas (postures), various Kumbhakas, and other divine means, all should be practised in the practice of Hatha Yoga, till the fruit—Râja Yoga—is obtained.

ॐ

iti haṭha-pradīpikāyāṃ prathamopadeśaḥ

End of chapter 1st, on the method of forming the Âsanas.

Chapter 2

Pranayamas

Dvitīyopadeśah

1.) athāsane dṝdhe yoghī vaśī hita-mitāśanaḥ I ghurūpadiṣhṭa-mārgheṇa prāṇāyāmānsam-abhyaset

Posture becoming established, a Yogî, master of himself, eating salutary and moderate food, should practise Prânâyâma, as instructed by his guru.

2.) chale vāte chalaṃ chittaṃ niśchale niśchalaṃ bhavet II yoghī sthāṇutvamāpnoti tato vāyuṃ nirodhayet

Respiration being disturbed, the mind becomes disturbed. By restraining respiration, the Yogî gets steadiness of mind.

3.) yāvadvāyuḥ sthito dehe tāvajjīvanamuchy-ate I maraṇaṃ tasya niṣhkrāntistato vāyuṃ nirodhayet

So long as the (breathing) air stays in the body, it is called life. Death consists in the passing out of the (breathing) air. It is, therefore, necessary to restrain the breath.

4.) malākalāsu nāḍīṣhu māruto naiva madhyaghaḥ I kathaṃ syādunmanībhāvaḥ kārya-siddhiḥ kathaṃ bhavet

The breath does not pass through the middle channel (susumnâ), owing to the impurities of the nâdîs. How can then success be attained, and how can there be the unmanî avasthâ.

5.) śuddhameti yadā sarvaṃ nāḍī-chakraṃ malākulam I tadaiva jāyate yoghī prāṇa-saṃghrahaṇe kṣhamaḥ

When the whole system of nâdîs which is full of impurities, is cleaned, then the Yogî becomes able to control the Prâna.

6.) prāṇāyāmaṃ tataḥ kuryānnityaṃ sāttvikayā dhiyā I yathā suṣhumṇā-nāḍīsthā malāḥ śuddhiṃ prayānti cha

Therefore, Prânâyâma should be performed daily with sâtwika buddhi (intellect free from raja and tama or activity and sloth), in order to drive out the impurities of the susumnâ.

7+8.) baddha-padmāsano yoghī prāṇaṃ

chandreṇa pūrayet I dhārayitvā yathā-śakti bhūyaḥ sūryeṇa rechayet

prāṇaṃ sūryeṇa chākṝṣhya pūrayedudaraṃ śanaiḥ I vidhivatkumbhakaṃ kṛtvā punaśch-andreṇa rechayet

Method of performing Prânâyâma.

Sitting in the Padmâsana posture the Yogî should fill in the air through the left nostril (closing the right one); and, keeping it confined according to one's ability, it should be expelled slowly through the sûrya (right nostril). Then, drawing in the air through the sûrya (right nostril) slowly, the belly should be filled, and after performing Kumbhaka as before, it should be expelled slowly through the chandra (left nostril).

9.) yena tyajettena pītvā dhārayedatirodha-taḥ I rechayechcha tato|anyena śanaireva na veghataḥ

Inhaling thus through the one, through which it was expelled, and having restrained it there, till possible, it should be exhaled through the other, slowly and not forcibly.

10.) prāṇaṃ chediḍayā pibenniyamitaṃ bhūyo I anyathā rechayet pītvā pingghalayā samīraṇamatho baddhvā tyajedvāmayā I sūrya-chandramasoranena vidhinābhyāsaṃ sadā tanvatāṃ śuddhā nāḍi-ghaṇā bhavanti yamināṃ māsa-trayādūrdhvataḥ

If the air be inhaled through the left nostril, it should be expelled again through the other, and filling it through the right nostril, confining it there, it should be expelled through the left nostril. By practising in this way, through the right and the left nostrils alternately, the whole of the collection of the nâdîs of the yamîs (practisers) becomes clean, i.e., free from impurities, after 3 months and over.

11.) prātarmadhyandine sāyamardha-rātre cha kumbhakān I śanairaśīti-paryantaṃ chatur-vāraṃ samabhyaset

Kumbhakas should be performed gradually 4 times during day and night, i.e., (morning, noon, evening and midnight), till the number of Kumbhakas for one time is 80 and for day and night together it is 320.

12.) kanīyasi bhavedsveda kampo bhavati madhyame I uttame sthānamāpnoti tato vāy-uṃ nibandhayet

In the beginning there is perspiration, in the middle stage there is quivering, and in the last or the 3rd stage one obtains steadiness; and then the breath should be made steady or motionless.

13.) jalena śrama-jātena ghātra-mardanamācharet I dṝḍhatā laghutā chaiva tena ghātrasya jāyate

The perspiration exuding from exertion of practice should be rubbed into the body (and not wiped), as by so doing the body becomes strong.

14.) abhyāsa-kāle prathame śastaṃ kṣhīrājya-bhojanam I tato|abhyāse dṝḍhībhūte na tādṝng-niyama-ghrahaḥ

During the first stage of practice the food consisting of milk and ghee is wholesome. When the practice becomes established, no such restriction is necessary.

15.) yathā siṃho ghajo vyāghro bhavedvaśyaḥ śanaiḥ śanaiḥ I tathaiva sevito vāyuranyathā hanti sādhakam

Just as lions, elephants and tigers are controlled by and by, so the breath is controlled by slow degrees, otherwise (i.e., by being hasty or using too much force) it kills the practiser himself.

16.) prāṇāyāmena yuktena sarva-rogha-kṣhayo bhavet I ayuktābhyāsa-yoghena sarva-rogha-samudghamaḥ

When Prânayama, etc., are performed properly, they eradicate all diseases; but an improper practice generates diseases.

17.) hikkā śvāsaścha kāsaścha śiraḥ-karṇākṣhi-vedanāḥ I bhavanti vividhāḥ roghāḥ pavanasya prakopataḥ

Hiccough, asthma, cough, pain in the head, the ears, and the eyes; these and other various kinds of diseases are generated by the disturbance of the breath.

18.) yuktaṃ yuktaṃ tyajedvāyuṃ yuktaṃ yuktaṃ cha pūrayet I yuktaṃ yuktaṃ cha badhnīyādevaṃ siddhimavāpnuyāt

The air should be expelled with proper tact and should be filled in skilfully; and when it has been kept confined properly it brings success.

NB.—The above caution is necessary to warn the aspirants against omitting any instruction; and, in their zeal to gain success or siddhis early, to begin the practice, either by using too much force in filling in, confining and expelling the air, or by omitting any instructions, it may cause unnecessary pressure on their ears, eyes, &c,, and cause pain. Every word in the instructions is full of meaning and is necessarily used in the slokas, and should be followed very carefully and with due attention. Thus there will be nothing to fear whatsoever. We are inhaling and exhaling the air throughout our lives without any sort of danger, and Prânayama being only a regular form of it, there should be no cause to fear.

19.) yadā tu nāḍī-śuddhiḥ syāttathā chihnāni bāhyataḥ I kāyasya kṝśatā kāntistadā jāyate niśchitam

When the nâdîs become free from impurities, and there appear the outward signs of success, such as lean body and glowing colour, then one should feel certain of success.

20.) yatheṣhṭaṃ dhāraṇaṃ vāyoranalasya pradīpanam I nādābhivyaktirāroghyaṃ jāyate nāḍi-śodhanāt

By removing the impurities, the air can be restrained, according to one's wish and the appetite is increased, the divine sound is awakened, and the body becomes healthy.

21.) meda-śleṣhmādhikaḥ pūrvaṃ ṣhaṭ-karmāṇi samācharet I anyastu nācharettāni doṣhāṇāṃ samabhāvataḥ

If there be excess of fat or phlegm in the body, the six kinds of kriyâs (duties) should be performed first. But others, not suffering from the excess of these, should not perform them.

22.) dhautirbastistathā netistrāṭakaṃ nau-likaṃ tathā I kapāla-bhātiśchaitāni ṣhaṭ-karmāṇi prachakṣhate

The six kinds of duties are: Dhauti, Basti, Neti, Trâtaka, Nauti and Kapâla Bhâti. These are called the six actions.

23.) karma ṣhaṭkamidaṃ ghopyaṃ ghaṭa-śod-hana-kārakam I vichitra-ghuṇa-sandhāya pūjyate yoghi-pungghavaiḥ

These six kinds of actions which cleanse the body should be kept secret. They produce extraordinary attributes and are performed with earnestness by the best of Yogîs.

24.) tatra dhautiḥ
chatur-angghula-vistāraṃ has-ta-pañcha-daśāyatam I ghurūpadiṣhṭa-mārg-heṇa siktaṃ vastraṃ śanairghraset I punaḥ pratyāharechchaitaduditaṃ dhauti-karma tat

The Dhauti.

A strip of cloth, about 3 inches wide and 15 cubits long, is pushed in (swallowed), when moist with warm water, through the passage shown by the guru, and is taken out again. This is called Dhauti Karma.

NB.—The strip should be moistened with a little warm water, and the end should be held with the teeth. It is swallowed slowly, little by little; thus, first day 1 cubit, 2nd day 2 cubits, 3rd day 3 cubits, and so on. After swallowing it the stomach should be given a good, round motion from left to right, and then it should be taken out slowly and gently.

25.) kāsa-śvāsa-plīha-kuṣhṭhaṃ kapharog-hāścha viṃśatiḥ I dhauti-karma-prabhāveṇa prayāntyeva na saṃśayaḥ

There is no doubt, that cough, asthma, enlargement of the spleen, leprosy, and 20 kinds of diseases born of phlegm, disappear by the practice of Dhauti Karma.

26.) atha bastiḥ

nābhi-daghna-jale pāyau nyasta-nālotkaṭās-anaḥ I ādhārākuñchanaṃ kuryātkṣhālanaṃ basti-karma tat

The Basti.

Squatting in navel-deep water, and introducing a six inches long, smooth piece of ½ an inch diameter pipe, open at both ends, half inside the anus; it (anus) should he drawn up (contracted) and then expelled. This washing is called the Basti Karma.

27.) ghulma-plīhodaraṃ chāpi vāta-pitta-kap-hodbhavāḥ I basti-karma-prabhāveṇa kṣhīy-ante sakalāmayāḥ

By practising this Basti Karma, colic, enlarged spleen, and dropsy, arising from the disorders of Vâta (air), pitta (bile) and kapha (phlegm), are all cured.

28.) dhāntvadriyāntaḥ-karaṇa-prasādaṃ dadhāchcha kāntiṃ dahana-pradīptam I aśeṣha-doṣhopachayaṃ nihanyād abhyasy-amānaṃ jala-basti-karma

By practising Basti with water, the Dhâtâs, the Indriyas

and the mind become calm. It gives glow and tone to the body and increases the appetite. All the disorders disappear.

29.) atha netiḥ
sūtraṃ vitasti-susnighdhaṃ nāsānāle pra-veśayet I mukhānnirghamayechchaiṣhā netiḥ siddhairnighadyate

The Neti.

A cord made of threads and about six inches long, should be passed through the passage of the nose and the end taken out in the mouth. This is called by adepts the Neti Karma.

30.) kapāla-śodhinī chaiva divya-dṛṣhṭi-pradāyinī I jatrūrdhva-jāta-roghaughaṃ netirāśu nihanti cha

The Neti is the cleaner of the brain and giver of divine sight. It soon destroys all the diseases of the cervical and scapular regions.

31.) atha trāṭakam
nirīkṣhenniśchala-dṛśā sūkṣhma-lakṣhyaṃ samāhitaḥ I aśru-sampāta-paryantamāchāry-aistrāṭakaṃ smṛtam

The Trâtaka.

Being calm, one should gaze steadily at a small mark, till eyes are filled with tears. This is called Trataka by âchâryas.

32.) mochanaṃ netra-roghāṇāṃ tandādrīṇāṃ kapāṭakam I yatnatastrāṭakaṃ ghopyaṃ yathā hāṭaka-peṭakam

Trâtaka destroys the eye diseases and removes sloth, etc. It should be kept secret very carefully, like a box of jewellery.

33.) atha nauliḥ
amandāvarta-veghena tundaṃ savyāpasavya-taḥ I natāṃso bhrāmayedeṣhā nauliḥ sidd-haiḥ praśasyate

The Nauli.

Sitting on the toes with heels raised above the ground, and the palms resting on the ground, and in this bent posture the belly is moved forcibly from left to right just, as in vomiting. This is called by adepts the Nauli Karma.

34.) mandāghni-sandīpana-pāchanādi-sandhāpikānanda-karī sadaiva I aśeṣha-doṣha-maya-śoṣhaṇī cha haṭha-kriyā mauliriyaṃ cha nauliḥ

It removes dyspepsia, increases appetite and digestion, and is like the goddess of creation, and causes happiness. It dries up all the disorders. This Nauli is an excellent exercise in Hatha Yoga.

35.) atha kapālabhātiḥ
bhastrāvalloha-kārasya recha-pūrau sasambhramau I kapālabhātirvikhyātā kapha-doṣha-viśoṣhaṇī

The Kapâla Bhâti.

When inhalation and exhalation are performed very quickly, like a pair of bellows of a blacksmith, it dries up all the disorders from the excess of phlegm, and is known as Kapâla Bhâti.

36.) ṣhaṭ-karma-nirghata-sthaulya-kapha-doṣha-malādikaḥ I prāṇāyāmaṃ tataḥ kuryādanāyāsena siddhyati

When Prânâyâma is performed after getting rid of

obesity born of the defects phlegm, by the performance of the six duties, it easily brings success.

37.) prāṇāyāmaireva sarve praśuṣhyanti malā iti I āchāryāṇāṃ tu keṣhāṃchidanyatkarma na saṃmatam

Some âchâryâs (teachers) do not advocate any other practice, being of opinion that all the impurities are dried up by the practice of Prânâyâma.

38.) atha ghaja-karaṇī udara-ghata-padārthamudvamanti pavana-mapānamudīrya kaṇṭha-nāle I krama-pa-richaya-vaśya-nāḍi-chakrā ghaja-karaṇīti nighadyate haṭhajñaiḥ

Gaja Karani.

By carrying the Apâna Vâyû up to the throat, the food, etc., in the stomach are vomited. By degrees, the system of Nâdîs (Śankhinî) becomes known. This is called in Hatha as Gaja Karani.

39.) brahmādayo|api tridaśāḥ pavanābhyā-sa-tatparāḥ I abhūvannantaka-bhyāttasmāt-pavanamabhyaset

Brahmâ, and other Devas were always engaged in the exercise of Prânâyâma, and, by means of it, got rid of the fear of death. Therefore, one should practise prânâyâma regularly.

40.) yāvadbaddho marud-deśe yāvachchittaṃ nirākulam I yāvaddṛṣhṭirbhruvormadhye tāvatkāla-bhayaṃ kutaḥ

So long as the breath is restrained in the body, so long as the mind is undisturbed, and so long as the gaze is fixed between the eyebrows, there is no fear from Death.

41.) vidhivatprāṇa-saṃyāmairnāḍī-chakre viśodhite I suṣhumṇā-vadanaṃ bhittvā sukhādviśati mārutaḥ

When the system of Nâdis becomes clear of the impurities by properly controlling the prâna, then the air, piercing the entrance of the Suśumnâ, enters it easily.

42.) atha manonmanī

mārute madhya-saṃchāre manaḥ-sthairyaṃ prajāyate I yo manaḥ-susthirī-bhāvaḥ saivāvasthā manonmanī

Manomanî.

Steadiness of mind comes when the air moves Freely in the middle. That is the manonmanî condition, which is attained when the mind becomes calm.

43.) tat-siddhaye vidhānajñāśchitrānkurvanti kumbhakān I vichitra kumbhakābhyāsād-vichitrāṃ siddhimāpnuyāt

To accomplish it, various Kumbhakas are performed by those who are expert in the methods; for, by the practice of different Kumbhakas, wonderful success is attained.

44.) atha kumbhaka-bhedāḥ sūrya-bhedanamujjāyī sītkārī śītalī tathā I bhastrikā bhrāmarī mūrchchā plāvinīty-aṣhṭa-kumbhakāḥ

Different hinds of Kumbhakas. Kumbhakas are of eight kinds, viz., Sûrya Bhedan, Ujjâyî, Sîtkarî, Sîtalî, Bhastrikâ, Bhrâmarî, Mûrchhâ, and Plâvinî.

45.) pūrakānte tu kartavyo bandho jālandharābhidhaḥ I kumbhakānte rechakādau kartavyastūḍḍiyānakaḥ

At the end of Pûraka, Jâlandhara Bandha should be performed, and at the end of Kumbhaka, and at the beginning of Rechaka, Uddiyâna Bandha should be performed.

NB.—Pûraka is filling in of the air from outside.

Kumbhaka is the keeping the air confined inside. Rechaka is expelling the confined air. The instructions for Puraka, Kumbhaka and Rechaka will be found at their proper place and should he carefully followed.

46.) adhastātkuñchanenāśu kaṇṭha-sangkochane kṝte I madhye paśchima-tānena syātprāṇo brahma-nāḍighaḥ

By drawing up from below (Mûla Bandha) and contracting the throat (Jâlandhara Bandha) and by pulling back the middle of the front portion of the body (i.e., belly), the Prâna goes to the Brahma Nâdî (Susumnâ).

The middle hole, through the vertebral column, through which the spinal cord passes, is called the Susumnâ Nâdî of the Yogîs. The two other sympathetic cords, one on each aide of the spinal cord, are called the Idâ and the Pingalâ Nâdîs. These will be described later on.

47.) āpānamūrdhvamutthāpya prāṇaṃ kaṇṭhādadho nayet I yoghī jarā-vimuktaḥ sanṣhoḍaśābda-vayā bhavet

By pulling up the Apâna Vâyu and by forcing the Prâna Vâyu down the throat, the Yogî, liberated from old age, becomes young, as it were 16 years old.

Note.

The seat of the Prâna is the heart; of the Apâna anus; of the Samâna the region about the navel; of the Udâna the throat; while the Vyâna moves throughout the body.

48.) atha sūrya-bhedanam
āsane sukhade yoghī baddhvā chaivāsanaṃ tataḥ I dakṣha-nāḍyā samākṝṣhya bahiḥst-haṃ pavanaṃ śanaiḥ

Sûrya Bhedana.

Taking any comfortable posture and performing the âsana, the Yogî should draw in the air slowly, through the right nostril.

49.) ākeśādānakhāghrāchcha nirodhāvad-hi kumbhayet I tataḥ śanaiḥ savya-nāḍyā rechayetpavanaṃ śanaiḥ

Then it should be confined within, so that it fills from the nails to the tips of the hair, and then let out through the left nostril slowly.

Note. This is to be done alternately with both the nostrils, drawing in through the one, expelling through the other, and vice versa.

50.) kapāla-śodhanaṃ vāta-doṣha-ghnaṃ kṝmi-doṣha-hṝt I punaḥ punaridaṃ kāryaṃ sūrya-bhedanamuttamam

This excellent Sûrya Bhedana cleanses the forehead (frontal sinuses), destroys the disorders of Vâta, and removes the worms, and, therefore, it should be performed again and again.

Note.

Translation: I am going to describe the procedure of the practice of Yoga, in order that Yogîs may succeed. A wise man should leave his bed in the Usâ Kâla (i.e. at the peep of dawn or 4 o'clock) in the morning. 1.

Remembering his guru over his head, and his desired deity in his heart, after answering the calls of nature, and cleaning his mouth, he should apply Bhasma (ashes). 2.

In a clean spot, clean room and charming ground, he should spread a soft âsana (cloth for sitting on). Having seated on it and remembering, in his mind his guru and his God. 3.

Having extolled the place and the time and taking up the vow thus: 'To day by the grace of God, I will perform Prânâyâmas with âsanas for gaining samâdhi (trance) and its fruits.' He should salute the infinite Deva, Lord of the Nâgas, to ensure success in the âsanas (postures). 4.

Salutation to the Lord of the Nâgas, who is adorned with thousands of heads, set with brilliant jewels (manis), and who has sustained the whole universe, nourishes it, and is infinite. After this he should begin his exercise of âsanas and when fatigued, he should practise Śava âsana. Should there be no fatigue, he should not practise it. 5.

Before Kumbhaka, he should perform Viparîta Karnî mudrâ, in order that he may be able to perform Jâlandhar bandha comfortably. 6.

Sipping a little water, he should begin the exercise of Prânâyâma, after saluting Yogindras, as described in the Karma Parana, in the words of Śiva. 7.

Such as "Saluting Yogindras and their disciples and gurû Vinâyaka, the Yogî should unite with me with composed mind." 8.

While practising, he should sit with Siddhâsana, and having performed bandha and Kumbhaka, should begin with 10 Prânâyâmas the first day, and go on increasing 5 daily. 9.

With composed mind 80 Kumbhakas should be performed at a time; beginning first with the chandra (the left nostril) and then sûrya (the right nostril). 10.

This has been spoken of by wise men as Aouloma and Viloma. Having practised Sûrya Bhedan, with Bandhas, the wise rust) should practise Ujjâyî and then Sîtkârî Śîtalî, and Bhastrikâ, he may practice others or not. 11-12.

He should practise mudrâs properly, as instructed by his guru. Then sitting with Padmâsana, he should hear anâhata nâda attentively. 13.

He should resign the fruits of all his practice reverently to God, and, on rising on the completion of the practice, a warm bath should be taken. 14.

The bath should bring all the daily duties briefly to an end. At noon also a little rest should be taken at the end of the exercise, and then food should be taken. 15.

Yogîs should always take wholesome food and never anything unwholesome. After dinner he should eat Ilâchî or lavanga. 16.

Some like camphor, and betel leaf. To the Yogîs, practising Prânâyâma, betel leaf without powders, i, e., lime, nuts and kâtha, is beneficial. 17.

After taking food he should read books treating of salvation, or hear Purânas and repeat the name of God. 18. In the evening the exercise should be begun after finishing sandyhâ, as before, beginning the practice 3 ghatikâ or one hour before the sun sets. 19.

Evening sandhyâ should always be performed after practice, and Hatha Yoga should be practised at midnight. 20.

Viparîta Karni is to be practised in the evening and at midnight, and not just after eating, as it does no good at this time. 21.

51.) atha ujjāyī
mukhaṃ saṃyamya nāḍībhyāmākṝṣhya pavanaṃ śanaiḥ I yathā laghati kaṇṭhāttu hṝdayāvadhi sa-svanam

Ujjâyî.

Having closed the opening of the Nâdî (Larynx), the air should be drawn in such a way that it goes touching from the throat to the chest, and making noise while passing.

52.) pūrvavatkumbhayetprāṇaṃ rechayediḍayā tathā I śleṣhma-doṣha-haraṃ kaṇṭhe dehānala-vivardhanam

It should be restrained, as before, and then let out through Idâ (the left nostril). This removes ślesmâ (phlegm) in the throat and increases the appetite.

53.) nāḍī-jalodarādhātu-ghata-doṣha-vināśanam I ghachchatā tiṣhṭhatā kāryamujjāyyākhyaṃ tu kumbhakam

It destroys the defects of the nâdîs, dropsy and disorders of Dhâtu (humours). Ujjâyî should be performed in all conditions of life, even while walking or sitting.

54.) atha sītkārī

sītkāṃ kuryāttathā vaktre ghrāṇenaiva vijṝm-bhikām I evamabhyāsa-yoghena kāma-devo dvitīyakaḥ

Sîtkârî.

Sîtkârî is performed by drawing in the air through the mouth, keeping the tongue between the lips. The air thus drawn in should not be expelled through the mouth. By practising in this way, one becomes next to the God of Love in beauty.

55.) yoghinī chakra-saṃmānyaḥ sṝṣhṭi-saṃhāra-kārakaḥ I na kṣhudhā na tṝṣhā nidrā naivālasyaṃ prajāyate

He is regarded adorable by the Yoginîs and becomes the destroyer of the cycle of creation, He is not afflicted with hunger, thirst, sleep or lassitude.

56.) bhavetsattvaṃ cha dehasya sarvopadra-va-varjitaḥ I anena vidhinā satyaṃ yoghīnd-ro bhūmi-maṇḍale

The Satwa of his body becomes free from all the distur-bances. In truth, he becomes the lord of the Yogîs in this world.

57.) atha śītalī
jihvayā vāyumākṝṣhya pūrvavatkumbha-sādhanam I śanakairghrāṇa-randhrābhyāṃ rechayetpavanaṃ sudhīḥ

Śîtalî.

As in the above (Sîtkári), the tongue to be protruded a little out of the lips, when the air is drawn in. It is kept confined, as before, and then expelled slowly through the nostrils.

58.) ghulma-plīhādikānroghānjvaraṃ pittaṃ kṣhudhāṃ tṝṣhām I viṣhāṇi śītalī nāma kumbhikeyaṃ nihanti hi

This Śîtalî kumbhikâ cures colic, (enlarged) spleen, fever, disorders of bile, hunger, thirst, and counteracts poisons.

59.) atha bhastrikā
ūrvorupari saṃsthāpya śubhe pāda-tale ubhe I padmāsanaṃ bhavedetatsarva-pāpa-praṇāśanam

The Bhastrikâ.

The Padma Âsana consists in crossing the feet and

placing them on both the thighs; it is the destroyer of all sins.

60.) samyakpadmāsanaṃ baddhvā sama-ghrīvodaraḥ sudhīḥ I mukhaṃ saṃyamya yatnena prāṇaṃ ghrāṇena rechayet

Binding the Padma-Âsana and keeping the body straight, closing the mouth carefully, let the air be expelled through the nose.

61.) yathā laghati hṝt-kaṇṭhe kapālāvadhi sa-svanam I veghena pūrayechchāpi hṝt-padmāvadhi mārutam

It should be filled up to the lotus of the heart, by drawing it in with force, making noise and touching the throat, the chest and the head.

62.) punarvirechayettadvatpūrayechcha punaḥ punaḥ I yathaiva lohakāreṇa bhastrā veghena chālyate

It should he expelled again and filled again and again as before, just as a pair of bellows of the blacksmith is worked.

63.) tathaiva sva-śarīra-sthaṃ chālayetpava-naṃ dhiyā I yadā śramo bhaveddehe tadā sūryeṇa pūrayet

In the same way, the air of the body should be moved intelligently, filling it through Sûrya when fatigue is experienced.

64.) yathodaraṃ bhavetpūrṇamanilena tathā laghu I dhārayennāsikāṃ madhyā-tar-janībhyāṃ vinā dṛḍham

The air should be drawn in through the right nostril by pressing the thumb against the left side of the nose, so as to close the left nostril; and when filled to the full, it should be closed with the fourth finger (the one next to the little finger) and kept confined.

65.) vidhivatkumbhakaṃ kṛtvā rechayediḍay-ānilam I vāta-pitta-śleṣhma-haraṃ śarīrāgh-ni-vivardhanam

Having confined it properly, it should be expelled through the Idâ (left nostril). This destroys Vâta, pitta (bile) and phlegm and increases the digestive power (the gastric fire).

66.) kuṇḍalī bodhakaṃ kṣhipraṃ pavanaṃ sukhadaṃ hitam I brahma-nāḍī-mukhe saṃstha-kaphādy-arghala-nāśanam

It quickly awakens the Kundalinî, purifies the system, gives pleasure, and is beneficial. It destroys phlegm and the impurities accumulated at the entrance of the Brahma Nâdî.

67.) samyaghghātra-samudbhūta-ghranthi-traya-vibhedakam I viśeṣheṇaiva kartavyam bhastrākhyaṃ kumbhakaṃ tvidam

This Bhastrikâ should be performed plentifully, for it breaks the three knots: Brahma granthi (in the chest), Visnu granthi (in the throat), and Rudra granthi (between the eyebrows) of the body.

68.) atha bhrāmarī
veghādghoṣhaṃ pūrakaṃ bhṝnggha-nādaṃ bhṝngghī-nādaṃ rechakaṃ manda-mandam I yoghīndrāṇamevamabhyāsa-yoghāch chitte jātā kāchidānanda-līlā

The Bhrâmari.

By filling the air with force, making noise like Bhringi

(wasp), and expelling it slowly, making noise in the same way; this practice causes a sort of ecstacy in the minds of Yogîndras.

69.) atha mūrchchā
pūrakānte ghāḍhataraṃ baddhvā jālandharaṃ śanaiḥ I rechayenmūrchchākhyeyaṃ mano-mūrchchā sukha-pradā

The Mûrchhâ.

Closing the passages with Jâlandhar Bandha firmly at the end of Pûraka, and expelling the air slowly, is called Mûrchhâ, from its causing the mind to swoon and giving comfort.

70.) atha plāvinī
antaḥ pravartitodāra-mārutāpūritodaraḥ I payasyaghādhe|api sukhātplavate padma-patravat

The Plâvinî.

When the belly is filled with air and the inside of the body is filled to its utmost with air, the body floats on the deepest water, like the leaf of a lotus.

71.) prāṇāyāmastridhā prokto recha-pūra-ka-kumbhakaiḥ I sahitaḥ kevalaścheti kum-bhako dvividho mataḥ

Considering Pûraka (Filling), Rechaka (expelling) and Kumbhaka (confining), Prânâyâma is of three kinds, but considering it accompanied by Pûraka and Rechaka, and without these, it is of two kinds only, i.e., Sahita (with) and Kevala (alone).

72.) yāvatkevala-siddhiḥ syātsahitaṃ tāvada-bhyaset I rechakaṃ pūrakaṃ muktvā suk-haṃ yadvāyu-dhāraṇam

Exercise in Sahita should be continued till success in Kevala is gained. This latter is simply confining the air with ease, without Rechaka and Pûraka.

73.) prāṇāyāmo|ayamityuktaḥ sa vai keva-la-kumbhakaḥ I kumbhake kevale siddhe recha-pūraka-varjite

In the practice of Kevala Prânâyâma when it can be performed successfully without Rechaka and Pûraka, then it is called Kevala Kumbhaka.

74.) na tasya durlabhaṃ kiṃchittriṣhu lokeṣhu vidyate I śaktaḥ kevala-kumbhena yatheṣhṭaṃ vāyu-dhāraṇāt

There is nothing in the three worlds which may be difficult to obtain for him who is able to keep the air confined according to pleasure, by means of Kevala Kumbhaka.

75.) rāja-yogha-padaṃ chāpi labhate nātra saṃśayaḥ I kumbhakātkuṇḍalī-bodhaḥ kuṇḍalī-bodhato bhavet I anarghalā suṣhumṇā cha haṭha-siddhiścha jāyate

He obtains the position of Râja Yoga undoubtedly. Kundalinî awakens by Kumbhaka, and by its awakening, Susumnâ becomes free from impurities.

76.) haṭhaṃ vinā rājayogho rāja-yoghaṃ vinā haṭhaḥ I na sidhyati tato yughmamāniṣhpatteḥ samabhyaset

No success in Râja Yoga without Hatha Yoga, and no success in Hatha Yoga without Râja Yoga. One should, therefore, practise both of these well, till complete success is gained.

77.) kumbhaka-prāṇa-rodhānte kuryāchchit-tam nirāśrayam I evamabhyāsa-yoghena rāja-yogha-padaṃ vrajet

On the completion of Kumbhaka, the mind should be given rest. By practising in this way one is raised to the position of (succeeds in getting) Râja Yoga.

78.) vapuḥ kṛśatvaṃ vadane prasannatā nā-da-sphuṭatvaṃ nayane sunirmale I aroghatā bindu-jayo|aghni-dīpanaṃ nāḍī-viśuddhir-haṭha-siddhi-lakṣhaṇam

Indications of success in the practice of Hatha Yoga.

When the body becomes lean, the face glows with delight, Anâhatanâda manifests, and eyes are clear, body is healthy, bindu under control, and appetite increases, then one should know that the Nâdîs are purified and success in Hatha Yoga is approaching.

ॐ

iti haṭha-pradīpikāyāṃ dvitīyopadeśaḥ

End of Chapter II.

Chapter 3

MUDRAS

Trtīyopadeśah

1.) sa-śaila-vana-dhātrīṇāṃ yathād-hāro|ahi-nāyakaḥ I sarveṣhāṃ yogha-tan-trāṇāṃ tathādhāro hi kuṇḍalī

As the chief of the snakes is the support of the earth with all the mountains and forests on it, so all the Tantras (Yoga practices) rest on the Kundalinî. (The Vertebral column.)

2.) suptā ghuru-prasādena yadā jāgharti kuṇḍalī I tadā sarvāṇi padmāni bhidyante ghranthayo|api cha

When the sleeping Kundalinî awakens by favour of a guru, then all the lotuses (in the six chakras or centres) and all the knots are pierced through.

3.) prāṇasya śūnya-padavī tadā rājapathāy-ate I tadā chittaṃ nirālambaṃ tadā kālasya vañchanam

Susumnâ (Sûnya Padavî) becomes a main road for the passage of Prâna, and the mind then becomes free from all connections (with its objects of enjoyments) and Death is then evaded.

4.) suṣhumṇā śūnya-padavī brahma-randhraḥ mahāpathaḥ I śmaśānaṃ śāmbhavī madhya-mārghaśchetyeka-vāchakāḥ

Susumnâ, Sunya Padavî, Brahma Randhra, Mahâ Patha, Śmaśâna, Śambhavî, Madhya Mârga, are names of one and the same thing.

5.) tasmātsarva-prayatnena prabodhayitumīśvarīm I brahma-dvāra-mukhe suptāṃ mudrābhyāsaṃsamācharet

In order, therefore, to awaken this goddess, who is sleeping at the entrance of Brahma Dwâra (the great door), mudrâs should be practised well.

6.) mahāmudrā mahābandho mahāvedhaścha khecharī I uḍḍīyānaṃ mūlabandhaścha bandho jālandharābhidhaḥ

The mudrâs.

Mahâ Mudrâ, Mahâ Bandha, Mahâ Vedha, Khecharî, Uddiyâna Bandha, Mûla Bandha, Jâlandhara Bandha.

7.) karaṇī viparītākhyā vajrolī śakti-chālanam I idaṃ hi mudrā-daśakaṃ jarā-maraṇa-nāśa-nam

Viparîta Karanî, Vajroli, and Śakti Châlana. These are the ten Mudrâs which annihilate old age and death.

8.) ādināthoditaṃ divyamaṣhṭaiśva-rya-pradāyakam I vallabhaṃ sarva-sidd-hānāṃ durlabhaṃ marutāmapi

They have been explained by Âdi Nâtha (Śiva) and give eight kinds of divine wealth. They are loved by all the Siddhas and are hard to attain even by the Marutas.

Note.—The eight Aiśwaryas are: Animâ (becoming small, like an atom), Mahimâ (becoming great, like âkâs, by drawing in atoms of Prakriti), Garimâ (light things, like cotton becoming very heavy like mountains.)

Prâpti (coming within easy reach of everything; as touching the moon with the little finger, while standing on the earth.)

Prâkâmya (non-resistance to the desires, as entering the earth like water.)

Îsatâ (mastery over matter and objects made of it.)

Vaśitwa (controlling the animate and inanimate objects.)

9.) ghopanīyaṃ prayatnena yathā ratna-karaṇḍakam I kasyachinnaiva vaktavyaṃ kula-strī-surataṃ yathā

These Mudrâs should be kept secret by every means, as one keeps one's box of jewellery, and should, on no account be told to any one, just as husband and wife keep their dealings secret.

10.) atha mahā-mudrā
pāda-mūlena vāmena yoniṃ sampīḍya dakṣhiṇām I prasāritaṃ padaṃ kṛtvā karābhyāṃ dhārayeddṛḍham

The mahâ mudrâ.

Pressing the Yoni (perineum) with the heel of the left foot, and stretching forth the right foot, its toe should be grasped by the thumb and first finger.

11+12.) kaṇṭhe bandhaṃ samāropya dhārayedvāyumūrdhvataḥ I yathā daṇḍa-hataḥ sarpo daṇḍākāraḥ prajāyate

ṛjvībhūtā tathā śaktiḥ kuṇḍalī sahasā bhavet I tadā sā maraṇāvasthā jāyate dvipuṭāśrayā

By stopping the throat (by Jâlandhara Bandha) the air is drawn in from the outside and carried down. Just as a snake struck with a stick becomes straight like a stick, in the same way, śakti (susumnâ) becomes straight at once. Then the Kundalinî, becoming as it were dead, and,

leaving both the Idâ and the Pingalâ, enters the susumnâ (the middle passage). 11-12.

13.) tataḥ śanaiḥ śanaireva rechayennaiva veghataḥ I mahā-mudrāṃ cha tenaiva vadanti vibudhottamāḥ

It should be expelled then, slowly only and not violently. For this very reason, the best of the wise men call it the Mahâ Mudrâ. This Mahâ Mudrâ has been propounded by great masters.

14.) iyaṃ khalu mahāmudrā mahā-siddhaiḥ pradarśitā I mahā-kleśādayo doṣhāḥ kṣhīyante maraṇādayaḥ I mahā-mudrāṃ cha tenaiva vadanti vibudhottamāḥ

Great evils and pains, like death, are destroyed by it, and for this reason wise men call it the Mahâ Mudrâ.

15.) chandrāngghe tu samabhyasya sūryāngghe punarabhyaset I yāvat-tulyā bhavetsangkhyā tato mudrāṃ visarjayet

Having practised with the left nostril, it should be practised with the right one; and, when the number on both sides becomes equal, then the mudrâ should be discontinued.

16.) na hi pathyamapathyaṃ vā rasāḥ sarve|api nīrasāḥ I api bhuktaṃ viṣhaṃ ghoraṃ pīyūṣhamapi jīryati

There is nothing wholesome or injurious; for the practice of this mudrâ destroys the injurious effects of all the rasas (chemicals). Even the deadliest of poisons, if taken, acts like nectar.

17.) kṣhaya-kuṣhṭha-ghudāvarta-ghulmājīrṇa-puroghamāḥ I tasya doṣhāḥ kṣhayaṃ yānti mahāmudrāṃ tu yo|abhyaset

Consumption, leprosy, prolapsus anii, colic, and the diseases due to indigestion, all these irregularities are removed by the practice of this Mahâ Mudrâ.

18.) kathiteyaṃ mahāmudrā mahā-siddhi-karā

nṝṇām I ghopanīyā prayatnena na deyā yasya kasyachit

This Mahâ Mudrâ has been described as the giver of great success (Siddhi) to men. It should be kept secret by every effort, and not revealed to any and everyone.

19.) atha mahā-bandhaḥ
pārṣhṇiṃ vāmasya pādasya yoni-sthāne niyojayet I vāmorūpari saṃsthāpya dakṣhiṇaṃ charaṇaṃ tathā

The Mahâ Bandha.

Press the left heel to the perineum and place the right foot on the left thigh.

20.) pūrayitvā tato vāyuṃ hṝdaye chubukaṃ dṝḍham I niṣhpīḍyaṃ vāyumākuñchya mano-madhye niyojayet

Fill in the air, keeping the chin firm against the chest, and, having pressed the air, the mind should he fixed on the middle of the eyebrows or in the susumnâ (the spine).

21.) dhārayitvā yathā-śakti rechayedani-lamṃ śanaiḥ I savyāngghe tu samabhyasya dakṣhāngghe punarabhyaset

Having kept it confined so long as possible, it should be expelled slowly. Having practised on the left side, it should be practised on the right side.

22.) matamatra tu keṣhāṃchitkaṇṭha-band-haṃ vivarjayet I rāja-danta-stha-jihvāyā bandhaḥ śasto bhavediti

Some are of opinion that the closing of throat is not necessary here, for keeping the tongue pressed against the roots of the upper teeth makes a good bandha (stop).

23.) ayaṃ tu sarva-nāḍīnāmūrdhvaṃ gha-ti-nirodhakaḥ I ayaṃ khalu mahā-bandho mahā-siddhi-pradāyakaḥ

This stops the upward motion of all the Nâdîs. Verily this Mahâ Bandha is the giver of great Siddhis.

24.) kāla-pāśa-mahā-bandha-vimochana-vichakṣhaṇaḥ I triveṇī-sangghamaṃ dhatte kedāraṃ prāpayenmanaḥ

This Mahâ Bandha is the most skilful means for cutting away the snares of death. It brings about the conjunction of the Trivenî (Idâ, Pingalâ and Susumnâ) and carries the mind to Kedâr (the space between the eyebrows, which is the seat of Śiva).

25.) rūpa-lāvaṇya-sampannā yathā strī puruṣhaṃ vinā I mahā-mudrā-mahā-bandhau niṣhphalau vedha-varjitau

As beauty and loveliness, do not avail a woman without husband, so the Mahâ Mudrâ and the Mahâ-Bandha are useless without the Mahâ Vedha.

26.) atha mahā-vedhaḥ mahā-bandha-sthito yoghī kṝtvā pūrakame-ka-dhīḥ I vāyūnāṃ ghatimāvṝtya nibhṝtaṃ kaṇṭha-mudrayā

The Mahâ Vedha.

Sitting with Mahâ Bandha, the Yogî should fill in the air and keep his mind collected. The movements of the Vâyus (Prâna and Apâna) should be stopped by closing the throat.)

27.) sama-hasta-yugho bhūmau sphichau sanāḍayechchanaiḥ I puṭa-dvayamatikramya vāyuḥ sphurati madhyaghaḥ

Resting both the hands equally on the ground, he should raise himself a little and strike his buttocks against the ground gently. The air, leaving both the passages (Idâ and Pingalâ), starts into the middle one.

28.) soma-sūryāghni-sambandho jāyate chāmṛtāya vai I mṛtāvasthā samutpannā tato vāyuṃ virechayet

The union of the Idâ and the Pingalâ is effected, in order to bring about immortality. When the air becomes as it were dead (by leaving its course through the Idâ and the Pingalâ) (i.e., when it has been kept confined), then it should be expelled.

29.) mahā-vedho|ayamabhyāsānmahā-siddhi-pradāyakaḥ I valī-palita-vepa-ghnaḥ sevyate sādhakottamaiḥ

The practice of this Mahâ Vedha, the giver of great Siddhis, destroys old age, grey hair, and shaking of the body, and therefore it is practised by the best masters.

30.) etattrayaṃ mahā-ghuhyaṃ jarā-mṝtyu-vināśanam I vahni-vṝddhi-karaṃ chaiva hyaṇimādi-ghuṇa-pradam

These THREE are the great secrets. They are the destroyers of old age and death, increase the appetite, confer the accomplishments of Anima, etc.

31.) aṣhṭadhā kriyate chaiva yāme yāme dine dine I puṇya-saṃbhāra-sandhāya pāpaugha-bhiduraṃ sadā I samyak-śikṣhāvatāmevaṃ svalpaṃ prathama-sādhanam

They should, be practised in 8 ways, daily and hourly. They increase collection of good actions and lessen the evil ones. People, instructed well, should begin their practice, little by little, first.

32.) atha khecharī
kapāla-kuhare jihvā praviṣhṭā viparītaghā I bhruvorantarghatā dṝṣhṭirmudrā bhavati khecharī

The Khechari.

The Khechari Mudrâ is accomplished by thrusting the tongue into the gullet, by turning it over itself, and keeping the eyesight in the middle of the eyebrows.

33.) chedana-chālana-dohaiḥ kalāṃ kra-meṇātha vardhayettāvat I sā yāvad-bhrū-madhyaṃ spṛśati tadā khecharī-siddhiḥ

To accomplish this, the tongue is lengthened by cutting the frænum linguæ, moving, and pulling it. When it can touch the space between the eyebrows, then Khechari can be accomplished.

34.) snuhī-patra-nibhaṃ śastraṃ sutīkṣhṇaṃ snighdha-nirmalam I samādāya tatastena roma-mātraṃ samuchchinet

Taking a sharp, smooth, and clean instrument, of the shape of a cactus leaf, the frænum of the tongue should be cut a little (as much as a hair's thickness), at a time.

35.) tataḥ saindhava-pathyābhyāṃ chūrṇitābhyāṃ pragharṣhayet I punaḥ sap-ta-dine prāpte roma-mātraṃ samuchchinet

Then rock salt and yellow myrobalan (both powdered) should be rubbed in. On the 7th day, it should again be cut a hair's breadth.

36.) evaṃ krameṇa ṣhaṇ-māsaṃ nityaṃ yuk-taḥ samācharet I ṣhaṇmāsādrasanā-mūla-śirā-bandhaḥ praṇaśyati

One should go on doing thus, regularly for six months. At the end of six months, the frænum of the tongue will be completely cut.

37.) kalāṃ parāngmukhīṃ kṝtvā tripathe pariyojayet I sā bhavetkhecharī mudrā vyoma-chakraṃ taduchyate

Turning the tongue upwards, it is fixed on the three ways (œsophagus, windpipe and palate.) Thus it makes the Khechari Mudrâ, and is called the Vyoma Chakra.

38.) rasanāmūrdhvaghāṃ kṝtvā kṣhaṇārdhamapi tiṣhṭhati I viṣhairvimuchyate yoghī vyādhi-mṝtyu-jarādibhiḥ

The Yogî who sits for a minute turning his tongue upwards, is saved from poisons, diseases, death, old age, etc.

39.) na rogho maraṇaṃ tandrā na nidrā na kṣhudhā tṝṣhā I na cha mūrchchā bhavettasya yo mudrāṃ vetti khecharīm

He who knows the Khechari Mudrâ is not afflicted with disease, death, sloth, sleep, hunger, thirst, and swooning.

40.) pīḍyate na sa roghеṇa lipyate na cha karmaṇā । bādhyate na sa kālena yo mudrāṃ vetti khecharīm

He who knows the Khechari Mudrâ, is not troubled by diseases, is not stained with karmas, and is not snared by time.

41.) chittaṃ charati khe yasmājjihvā charati khe ghatā । tenaiṣhā khecharī nāma mudrā siddhairnirūpitā

The Siddhas have devised this Khechari Mudrâ from the fact that the mind and the tongue reach âkâśa by its practice.

42.) khecharyā mudritaṃ yena vivaraṃ lambikordhvataḥ । na tasya kṣharate binduḥ kāminyāḥ śleṣhitasya cha

If the hole behind the palate be stopped with Khechari by turning the tongue upwards, then bindu cannot leave its place even if a woman were embraced.

43.) chalito|api yadā binduḥ samprāpto yoni-maṇḍalam । vrajatyūrdhvaṃ hṝtaḥ śaktyā nibaddho yoni-mudrayā

Even when there is movement of the bindu and it enters the genitals, it is seized by closing the perineum and is taken upward.

44.) ūrdhva-jihvaḥ sthiro bhūtvā somapānaṃ karoti yaḥ I māsārdhena na sandeho mṝtyuṃ jayati yoghavit

If the Yogî drinks Somarasa (juice) by sitting with the tongue turned backwards and mind concentrated, there is no doubt he conquers death within 15 days.

45.) nityaṃ soma-kalā-pūrṇaṃ śarīraṃ yasya yoghinaḥ I takṣhakeṇāpi daṣhṭasya viṣhaṃ tasya na sarpati

The yogi's body is forever full of the moon's nectar. Even if he is bitten by the king of snakes (Takshaka), he is not poisoned

46.) indhanāni yathā vahnistaila-varti cha dī-pakaḥ I tathā soma-kalā-pūrṇaṃ dehī dehaṃ na muñchati

Just as fuel kindles fire and oil a lamp, so the indweller of the body does not vacate while the body is full of the moon's nectar

47.) ghomāṃsaṃ bhakṣhayennityaṃ pibe-damara-vāruṇīm I kulīnaṃ tamahaṃ manye chetare kula-ghātakāḥ

By constant swallowing of the tongue he can drink amaravaruni. I consider him of high lineage (heritage). Others destroy the heritage.

48.) gho-śabdenoditā jihvā tatpraveśo hi tāluni I gho-māṃsa-bhakṣhaṇaṃ tattu mahā-pātaka-nāśanam

The word 'go' means tongue (and also means cow). When it enters into the upper palate, it is 'eating the flesh of the cow.' It (khechari) destroys the great sins.

49.) jihvā-praveśa-sambhūta-vahninotpāditaḥ khalu I chandrātsravati yaḥ sāraḥ sā syāda-mara-vāruṇī

When the tongue enters the cavity, indeed heat is produ-ced and the man's nectar flows.

50.) chumbantī yadi lambikāghramaniśaṃ jihvā-rasa-syandinī sa-kṣhārā kaṭukām-la-dughdha-sadṝśī madhvājya-tulyā tathā I vyādhīnāṃ haraṇaṃ jarānta-karaṇaṃ

śastrāghamodīraṇaṃ tasya syādamaratva-maṣhṭa-ghuṇitaṃ siddhāngghanākarṣhaṇam

When the tongue constantly presses the cavity, the moon's nectar (flows and) has a saline, pungent and acidic flavor. It is like (the consistency of) milk, ghee, honey. Fatal diseases, old age and weapons are warded off. From that, immortality and the eight siddhis or perfections manifest.

51.) ūrdvhāsyo rasanāṃ niyamya vivare śaktiṃ parāṃ chintayan I utkallola-kalā-jalaṃ cha vimalaṃ dhārāmayaṃ yaḥ piben nirvyādhiḥ sa mṝṇāla-komala-vapuryoghī chiraṃ jīvati

Fluid drips into the sixteen petalled lotus (vishuddhi chakra) when the tongue is inserted into the upper throat cavity; the paramshakti (kundalini) is released and one becomes concentrated in that (experience which ensues). The yogi who drinks the pure stream of nectar is freed from disease, has longevity, and has a body as soft and as beautiful as a lotus stem.

52.) yatprāleyaṃ prahita-suṣhiraṃ meru-mūrdhāntara-sthaṃ tasmiṃstattvaṃ pravadati sudhīstan-mukhaṃ nimnaghānām

I chandrātsāraḥ sravati vapuṣhastena mṝty-urnarāṇāṃ tadbadhnīyātsukaraṇamadho nānyathā kāya-siddhiḥ

The nectar is secreted from the topmost part of the Meru (Sushumna), the fountainhead of the nadis. He who has pure intellect can know the Truth therein. The nectar, which is the essence of the body, flows out from the moon and hence death ensues. Therefore khechari mudra should be practiced, otherwise perfection of the body cannot be attained.

53.) suṣhiraṃ jñāna-janakaṃ pañcha-sro-taḥ-samanvitam I tiṣhṭhate khecharī mudrā tasminśūnye nirañjane

Five nadis convene in this cavity and it is the source of knowledge. Khechari should be established in that void, untainted (by ignorance).

54.) ekaṃ sṝṣhṭimayaṃ bījamekā mudrā cha khecharī I eko devo nirālamba ekāvasthā manonmanī

There is only one seed of creation and one mudra – khechari; one deva independent of everything and one state – manonmani.

55.) atha uḍḍīyāna-bandhaḥ
baddho yena suṣhumṇāyāṃ prāṇastūḍḍīyate yataḥ I tasmāduḍḍīyanākhyo|ayaṃ yoghibhiḥ samudāhṝtaḥ

The Uddiyâna bandha.

Uddiyana bandha is so-called by the yogis because through its practice the prana (is concentrated at one point and) rises through sushumna.

56.) uḍḍīnaṃ kurute yasmādaviśrāntaṃ mahā-khaghaḥ I uḍḍīyānaṃ tadeva syāttava bandho|abhidhīyate

The bandha described is called the rising or flying bandha, because through its practice, the great bird (shakti) flies upward with ease.

57.) udare paśchimaṃ tānaṃ nābherūrdhvaṃ cha kārayet I uḍḍīyāno hyasau bandho mṝtyu-mātanggha-kesarī

Pulling the abdomen back in and making the navel rise is uddiyana bandha. It is the lion which conquers the elephant, death.

58.) uḍḍīyānaṃ tu sahajaṃ ghuruṇā kathitaṃ sadā I abhyasetsatataṃ yastu vṝddho|api taruṇāyate

Uddiyana is easy when practiced as told by the guru. Even an old person can become young when it is done regularly.

59.) nābherūrdhvamadhaśchāpi tānaṃ kuryātprayatnataḥ I ṣhaṇmāsamabhyasen-mṝtyuṃ jayatyeva na saṃśayaḥ

The region above and below the navel should be drawn backward with effort. There is no doubt that after six months of practice, death is conquered.

60.) sarveṣhāmeva bandhānāṃ uttamo hyuḍḍīyānakaḥ I uḍḍiyāne dṝḍhe bandhe muktiḥ svābhāvikī bhavet

Of all the bandhas, uddiyana is the best. Once it is mastered, mukti or liberation occurs spontaneously.

61.) atha mūla-bandhaḥ

pārṣhṇi-bhāghena sampīḍya yonimākuñchay-edghudam I apānamūrdhvamākṝṣhya mūla-bandho|abhidhīyate

The Moola bhanda.

Pressing the perineum/vagina with the heel and contracting the rectum so that the apana vayu moves upward is moola bandha.

62.) adho-ghatimapānaṃ vā ūrdhvaghaṃ kurute balāt I ākuñchanena taṃ prāhurmūla-bandhaṃ hi yoghinaḥ

By contracting the perineum the downward moving apana vayu is forced to go upward. Yogis call this moola bandha.

63.) ghudaṃ pārṣhṇyā tu sampīḍya vāyumākuñchayedbalāt I vāraṃ vāraṃ yathā chordhvaṃ samāyāti samīraṇaḥ

Press the heel firmly against the rectum and contract forcefully and repeatedly, so that the vital energy rises.

64.) prāṇāpānau nāda-bindū mūla-bandhena chaikatām I ghatvā yoghasya saṃsiddhiṃ yachchato nātra saṃśayaḥ

There is no doubt that by practicing moola bandha, prana/apana and nada/bindu are united, and total perfection attained.

65.) apāna-prāṇayoraikyaṃ kṣhayo mūtra-purīṣhayoḥ I yuvā bhavati vṛddho|api satataṃ mūla-bandhanāt

With constant practice of moola bandha, prana and apana unite, urine and stool are decreased and even an old person becomes young.

66.) apāna ūrdhvaghe jāte prayāte vah-ni-maṇḍalam I tadānala-śikhā dīrghā jāyate vāyunāhatā

Apana moves up into the region of fire (manipura chakra, the navel center), then the flames of the fire grow, being fanned by apana vayu.

67.) tato yāto vahny-apānau prāṇamuṣhṇa-svarūpakam I tenātyan-ta-pradīptastu jvalano dehajastathā

Then, when apana and the fin meet with prana, which is itself hot, the heat in the body is intensified.

68.) tena kuṇḍalinī suptā santaptā sampra-budhyate I daṇḍāhatā bhujangghīva niśvasya ṛjutāṃ vrajet

Through this, the sleeping kundalini is aroused by the extreme heat and it straightens itself just as a serpent beaten with a stick straightens and hisses.

69.) bilaṃ praviṣhṭeva tato brahma-nāḍyaṃ taraṃ vrajet I tasmānnityaṃ mūla-bandhaḥ kartavyo yoghibhiḥ sadā

Just as a snake enters its hole, so kundalini goes into brahma nadi. Therefore the yogi must always perform moola bandha.

70.) atha jalandhara-bandhaḥ kaṇṭhamākuñchya hṝdaye sthāpayechchibu-kaṃ dṝḍham I bandho jālandharākhyo|ayaṃ jarā-mṝtyu-vināśakaḥ

The Jâlandhara Bandha.

Contracting the throat by bringing the chin to the chest is the bandha called jalandhara. It destroys old age and death.

71.) badhnāti hi sirājālamadho-ghāmi nabho-jalam I tato jālandharo bandhaḥ kaṇṭha-duḥkhaugha-nāśanaḥ

That is jalandhara bandha which catches the flow of nectar in the throat. It destroys all throat ailments.

72.) jālandhare kṝte bandhe kaṇṭha-saṃko-cha-lakṣhaṇe I na pīyūṣhaṃ patatyaghnau na cha vāyuḥ prakupyati

Having done jalandhara bandha by contracting the throat, the nectar does not fall into the gastric fire and the prana is not agitated.

73.) kaṇṭha-saṃkochanenaiva dve nāḍyau stambhayeddṝḍham I madhya-chakramidaṃ jñeyaṃ ṣhoḍaśādhāra-bandhanam

The two Nâdîs should be stopped firmly by contracting the throat. This is called the middle circuit or centre (Madhya Chakra), and it stops the 16 âdhâras (i.e., vital parts).

Note.

The sixteen vital parts mentioned by renowned Yogîs are the (1) thumbs, (2) ankles, (3) knees, (4) thighs, (5) the prepuce, (6) organs of generation, (17) the navel, (8) the heart, (9) the neck, (10) the throat, (11) the palate, (12) the nose, (13) the middle of the eyebrows, (14) the forehead, (15) the head and (16) the Brahma randhra.

74.) mūla-sthānaṃ samākuñchya uḍḍiyānaṃ tu kārayet I iḍāṃ cha pingghalāṃ baddhvā vāhayetpaśchime pathi

By drawing up the mûlasthâna (anus,) Uddiyâna Bandha should be performed. The flow of the air should be directed to the Susumnâ, by closing the Idâ, and the Pingalâ. 73.

75.) anenaiva vidhānena prayāti pavano layam I tato na jāyate mṝtyurjarā-roghādikaṃ tathā

The Prâna becomes calm and latent by this means, and thus there is no death, old age, disease, etc.

76.) bandha-trayamidaṃ śreṣhṭhaṃ mahā-siddhaiścha sevitam I sarveṣhāṃ haṭha-tantrāṇāṃ sādhanaṃ yoghino viduḥ

These three Bandhas are the best of all and have been practised by the masters. Of all the means of success in the Hatha Yoga, they are known to the Yogîs as the chief ones.

77.) yatkiṃchitsravate chandrādamṝtaṃ divya-rūpiṇaḥ I tatsarvaṃ ghrasate sūryastena piṇḍo jarāyutaḥ

That nectar which flows from the moon has the quality of endowing enlightenment, but it is completely consumed by the sun, incurring old age.

78.) atha viparīta-karaṇī mudrā tatrāsti karaṇaṃ divyaṃ sūryasya mukha-vañchanam I ghurūpadeśato jñeyaṃ na tu śāstrārtha-koṭibhiḥ

The Viparîta Karani.

There is a wonderful means by which the nectar is averted from falling into the opening of the sun. This is obtained by the guru's instructions and not from the hundreds of shastras (treatises).

79.) ūrdhva-nābheradhastālorūrdhvaṃ bhānuradhaḥ śaśī I karaṇī viparītākhā ghuru-vākyena labhyate

With the navel region above and the palate below, the sun is above and the moon below. It is called vipareeta karani, the reversing process. When given by the guru's instructions it is fruitful.

80.) nityamabhyāsa-yuktasya jaṭharāghni-vivardhanī I āhāro bahulastasya sampādyaḥ sādhakasya cha

Digestion is strengthened by continual, regular practi-ce and therefore, the practitioner should always have sufficient food.

81.) alpāhāro yadi bhavedaghnirdahati tat-kṣhaṇāt I adhaḥ-śirāśchordhva-pādaḥ kṣhaṇaṃ syātprathame dine

If one takes only a little food, the heat produced by the digestion will destroy the system. Therefore, on the first day, one should only stay a moment with the feet up and head down.

82.) kṣhaṇāchcha kiṃchidadhikamabhya-sechcha dine dine I valitaṃ palitaṃ chaiva ṣhaṇmāsordhvaṃ na dṝśyate I yāma-mātraṃ tu yo nityamabhyasetsa tu kālajit

The practice should be done daily, gradually increasing the duration. After six months of practice, grey hairs and wrinkles become inconspicuous. One who practices it for yama (three hours conquers death.

83.) atha vajrolī
svechchayā vartamāno|api yoghoktairniy-amairvinā I vajrolīṃ yo vijānāti sa yoghī siddhi-bhājanam

The Vajrolî.

Even anyone living a free lifestyle without the formal rules of yoga, if he practices vajroli well, that yogi becomes a recipient of siddhis (perfections).

84.) tatra vastu-dvayaṃ vakṣhye durlabhaṃ yasya kasyachit I kṣhīraṃ chaikaṃ dvitīyaṃ tu nārī cha vaśa-vartinī

There are two things hard to obtain, one is milk and the second is a woman who can act according to your will.

85.) mehanena śanaiḥ samyaghūrdh-vākuñchanamabhyaset I puruṣho|apyathavā nārī vajrolī-siddhimāpnuyāt

By practicing gradual upward contractions during the emission in intercourse, any man or woman achieves perfection of vajroli.

86.) yatnataḥ śasta-nālena phūtkāraṃ vaj-ra-kandare I śanaiḥ śanaiḥ prakurvīta vāyu-saṃchāra-kāraṇāt

By slowly drawing in air through a prescribed tube inserted into the urethra of the penis, gradually air and prana traverse into the vajra kanda.

87.) nārī-bhaghe padad-bindumabhyāsenord-hvamāharet I chalitaṃ cha nijaṃ bindumūrd-hvamākṝṣhya rakṣhayet

The bindu (semen) that is about to fall into the woman's vagina should be made to move upwards with practice. And if it falls, the semen and the woman's fluid should be conserved by drawing it up.

88.) evaṃ saṃrakṣhayedbinduṃ jayati yoghavit I maraṇaṃ bindu-pātena jīvanaṃ bindu-dhāraṇāt

Therefore, the knower of yoga conquers death by preserving the bindu (semen). Release of the bindu means death; conservation of semen is life.

89.) sughandho yoghino dehe jāyate bin-du-dhāraṇāt I yāvadbinduḥ sthiro dehe tāvatkāla-bhayaṃ kutaḥ

As long as the bindu/semen is steady in the body, then where is the fear of death? The yogi's body smells pleasant by conserving the bindu/semen.

90.) chittāyattaṃ nṝṇāṃ śukraṃ śukrāyattaṃ cha jīvitam I tasmāchchukraṃ manaśchaiva rakṣhaṇīyaṃ prayatnataḥ

A man's semen can be controlled by the mind and control of semen is life giving. Therefore, his semen and mind should be controlled and conserved.

91.) ṝtumatyā rajo|apyevaṃ nijaṃ bindunṃ ch rakṣhayet I meḍhreṇākarṣhayedūrdhvaṃ samyaghabhyāsa-yogha-vit

The knower of yoga, perfect in the practice, conserves his bindu and the woman's rajas by drawing it up through the generative organ.

92.) atha sahajoliḥ sahajoliśchāmarolirvajrolyā bheda ekataḥ I jale subhasma nikṣhipya daghdha-gho-maya-sambhavam

The Sahajolî.

Sahajoli and amaroli are separate techniques of vajroli. The ashes of burnt cow manure should be mixed with water.

93.) vajrolī-maithunādūrdhvaṃ strī-puṃsoḥ svāńggha-lepanam I āsīnayoḥ sukhenaiva mukta-vyāpārayoḥ kṣhaṇāt

After performing vajroli during intercourse, (being in a comfortable position), the man and woman should wipe the ashes on specific parts of their bodies during the leisure time.

94.) sahajoliriyaṃ proktā śraddheyā yoghibhiḥ sadā I ayaṃ śubhakaro yogho bhogha-yukto|api muktidaḥ

It is called sahajoli and the yogis have complete faith in it. This is very beneficial and enables enlightenment through the combination of yoga and bhoga (sensual involvement).

95.) ayaṃ yoghaḥ puṇyavatāṃ dhīrāṇāṃ tattva-darśinām I nirmatsarāṇāṃ vai sidhyenna tu matsara-śālinām

Verily this yoga is perfected by virtuous and well-conducted men who have seen the truth and not those who are selfish.

96.) atha amarolī

pittolbaṇatvātprathamāmbu-dhārāṃ vihāya niḥsāratayāntyadhārām I niṣhevyate śītala-madhya-dhārā kāpālike khaṇḍamate|amarolī

The Amarolî.

According to the Kapalika sect, amaroli is practiced by drinking the cool midstream of urine. The first part of the urine is left as it contains bile, and the last part is left as it does not contain goodness.

97.) amarīṃ yaḥ pibennityaṃ nasyaṃ kurvandine dine I vajrolīmabhyasetsamyaksāmarolīti kathyate

One who drinks amari, takes it through the nose and practices vajroli, is said to be practicing amaroli.

98.) abhyāsānniḥsṝtāṃ chāndrīṃ vibhūtyā saha miśrayet I dhārayeduttamānggheṣhu divya-dṝṣhṭiḥ prajāyate

The practitioner should mix the semen with the ashes of burnt cow manure and wipe it on the upper parts of the body, it bestows divya drishti (clairvoyance or divine sight).

99.) puṃso binduṃ samākuñchya samyaghabhyāsa-pāṭavāt I yadi nārī rajo rakṣhedvajrolyā sāpi yoghinī

If a woman practices vajroli and saves her rajas and the man's bindu by thorough contraction, she is a yogini.

100.) tasyāḥ kiṃchidrajo nāśaṃ na ghachchati na saṃśayaḥ I tasyāḥ śarīre nādaścha bindutāmeva ghachchati

Without doubt, not even a little rajas is wasted through vajroli, the nada and bindu in the body become one.

101.) sa bindustadrajaśchaiva ekībhūya svadehaghau I vajroly-abhyāsa-yoghena sarva-siddhiṃ prayachchataḥ

The bindu and that rajas in one's own body unite through the union by practice of vajroli, thus bestowing all perfections or siddhis.

102.) rakṣhedākuñchanādūrdhvaṃ yā rajaḥ sā hi yoghinī I atītānāghataṃ vetti khecharī cha bhaveddhruvam

She is verily a yogini who conserves her rajas by contracting and raising it. She knows past, present and future and becomes fixed in khechari (i.e. consciousness moves into the higher realm).

103.) deha-siddhiṃ cha labhate vaj-roly-abhyāsa-yoghataḥ I ayaṃ puṇya-karo yogho bhoghe bhukte I api muktidaḥ

By the yoga of vajroli practice, perfection of the body fructifies. This auspicious yoga even brings liberation alongside with sensual involvement (bhoga).

104.) atha śakti-chālanam kuṭilāngghī kuṇḍalinī bhujangghī śaktirīśvarī I kuṇḍalyarundhatī chaite śabdāḥ pa-ryāya-vāchakāḥ

The Śakti châlana.

Kutilangi, kundalini, bhujangi, shakti, ishwari, kundali, arundhati are all synonymous terms.

105.) udghāṭayetkapāṭaṃ tu yathā kuṃchi-kayā haṭhāt I kuṇḍalinyā tathā yoghī mokṣhadvāraṃ vibhedayet

Just as a door is opened with a key, similarly the yogi opens the door to liberation with kundalini.

106.) yena mārgheṇa ghantavyaṃ brahma-st-hānaṃ nirāmayam I mukhenāchchādya tadvāraṃ prasuptā parameśvarī

The sleeping Parameshwari rests with her mouth closing that door, through which is the path to the knot of brahmasthana, the place beyond suffering.

107.) kandordhve kuṇḍalī śaktiḥ suptā mokṣhāya yoghinām I bandhanāya cha mūḍhānāṃ yastāṃ vetti sa yoghavit

The kundalini shakti sleeps above the kanda. This shakti is the means of liberation to the yogi and bondage for the ignorant.

One who knows this is the knower of yoga.

108.) kuṇḍalī kuṭilākārā sarpavatparikīrtitā | sā śaktiśchālitā yena sa mukto nātra saṃśayaḥ

Kundalini is said to be coiled like a snake. ***Without a doubt, one who makes that shakti flow obtains liberation.***

109.) ghangghā-yamunayormadhye bālaraṇḍāṃ tapasvinīm I balātkāreṇa ghṝhṇīyāttadviṣhṇoḥ paramaṃ padam

Between Ganga and Yamuna is the young widowed,

Balarandam practicing austerity. She should be seized forcibly, then one can reach the supreme state of Vishnu.

110.) iḍā bhaghavatī ghangghā pingghalā yamunā nadī I iḍā-pingghalayormadhye bālaraṇḍā cha kuṇḍalī

Ida is the holy Ganga, pingala the river Yamuna. Between ida and pingala in the middle is this young widow, kundalini.

111.) puchche praghṝhya bhujangghīṃ suptāmudbodhayechcha tām I nidrāṃ vihāya sā śaktirūrdhvamuttiṣhṭhate haṭhāt

By seizing the tail of kundalini serpent, she becomes very excited. Abandoning sleep that shakti is released and rises up.

112.) avasthitā chaiva phaṇāvatī sā prātaścha sāyaṃ praharārdha-mātram I prapūrya sūryātparidhāna-yuktyā praghṝhya nityaṃ parichālanīyā

Shakti Chalana Mudra.

Breathing in through the right nostril (pingala) the

serpent (shakti) should be seized through kumbhaka and rotated constantly for an hour and a half, morning and evening.

113.) ūrdhvaṃ vitasti-mātraṃ tu vistāraṃ chaturangghulam I mṛdulaṃ dhavalaṃ proktaṃ veṣhṭitāmbara-lakṣhaṇam

The kanda, situated above the anus, one hand span high and four fingers breath wide, is soft and white as if enveloped in cloth.

114.) sati vajrāsane pādau karābhyāṃ dhārayeddṛḍham I ghulpha-deśa-samīpe cha kandaṃ tatra prapīḍayet

Firmly seated in vajrasana, holding the ankles, one should squeeze the kanda close to the anus.

115.) vajrāsane sthito yoghī chālayitvā cha kuṇḍalīm I kuryādanantaraṃ bhastrāṃ kuṇḍalīmāśu bodhayet

In the position of vajrasana, the yogi should move the kundalini. Having done bhastrika pranayama the kundalini is soon aroused.

116.) bhānorākuñchanaṃ kuryātkuṇḍalīṃ chālayettataḥ I mṛtyu-vaktra-ghatasyāpi tasya mṛtyu-bhayaṃ kutaḥ

Contracting the sun in manipura, kundalini should be moved. Even if such a person should be on the verge of death, where is the need to fear death?

117.) muhūrta-dvaya-paryantaṃ nirbhay-aṃ chālanādasau I ūrdhvamākṛṣhyate kiṃchitsuṣhumṇāyāṃ samudghatā

By moving the kundalini fearlessly for an hour and a half, it is drawn into sushumna and rises up a little.

118.) tena kuṇḍalinī tasyāḥ suṣhumṇāyā mukhaṃ dhruvam I jahāti tasmātprāṇo|ayaṃ suṣhumṇāṃ vrajati svataḥ

In this way, it is easy for kundalini to issue from the opening of sushumna. Thus the prana proceeds through sushumna of its own accord.

119.) tasmātsaṃchālayennityaṃ sukha-suptā-marundhatīm I tasyāḥ saṃchālanenaiva yoghī roghaiḥ pramuchyate

In that way the sleeping kundalini should be regularly moved. By her regular movement, the yogi is freed from disease.

120.) yena saṃchālitā śaktiḥ sa yoghī siddhi-bhājanam I kimatra bahunoktena kālaṃ jayati līlayā

The yogi who moves the shakti regularly, enjoys perfection or siddhi. He easily conquers time and death. What more is there to say?

121.) brahmacharya-ratasyaiva nityaṃ hita-mitāśinaḥ I maṇḍalāddṛśyate siddhiḥ kuṇḍaly-abhyāsa-yoghinaḥ

One who enjoys being brahmacharya and always takes moderate diet and practices arousal of kundalini, achieves perfection in forty days.

122.) kuṇḍalīṃ chālayitvā tu bhastrāṃ kuryādviśeṣhataḥ I evamabhyasyato nityaṃ yamino yama-bhīḥ kutaḥ

Bhastrika pranayama with kumbhaka should specifically be practiced to activate kundalini. From where will the fear of death arise for a self- restrained practitioner who practices daily with regularity?

123.) dvā-saptati-sahasrāṇāṃ nāḍīnāṃ mala-śodhane I kutaḥ prakṣhālanopāyaḥ kuṇḍaly-abhyasanādṛte

What other methods are there to cleanse the 72,000 nadis of dirt besides the practice of arousing kundalini?

124.) iyaṃ tu madhyamā nāḍī dṛḍhābhyāsena yoghinām I āsana-prāṇa-saṃyāma-mudrābhiḥ saralā bhavet

This middle nadi, sushumna, easily becomes established, (straight) by the yogi's persistent practice of asana, pranayama, mudra and concentration.

125.) abhyāse tu vinidrāṇāṃ mano dhṛtvā samādhinā I rudrāṇī vā parā mudrā bhadrāṃ siddhiṃ prayachchati

For those who are alert and the mind one-pointed (disciplined) in samadhi, rudrani or shambhavi mudra is the greatest mudra for bestowing perfection.

126.) rāja-yoghaṃ vinā pṛthvī rāja-yoghaṃ vinā niśā I rāja-yoghaṃ vinā mudrā vichitrā-pi na śobhate

The earth without raja yoga, night without raja yoga, even the various mudras without raja yoga are useless, i.e. not beautiful.

127.) mārutasya vidhiṃ sarvaṃ mano-yuktaṃ samabhyaset I itaratra na kartavyā mano-vṝt-tirmanīṣhiṇā

All the pranayama methods are to be done with a concentrated mind. The wise man should not let his mind be involved in the modifications (vrittis).

128.) iti mudrā daśa proktā ādināthena śam-bhunā I ekaikā tāsu yamināṃ mahā-sidd-hi-pradāyinī

Thus the ten mudras have been told by Adinath, Shambhu. Each one is the bestower of perfection to the self-restrained.

129.) upadeśaṃ hi mudrāṇāṃ yo datte sāmpradāyikam I sa eva śrī-ghuruḥ svāmī sākṣhādīśvara eva saḥ

One who instructs mudra in the tradition of guru/disciple is the true guru and form of Ishwara.

130.) tasya vākya-paro bhūtvā mudrābhyā-se samāhitaḥ I aṇimādi-ghuṇaiḥ sārdhaṃ labhate kāla-vañchanam

By following explicitly his (guru's) words, and practicing mudra; one obtains the qualities of anima, etc. and overcomes death/time

ॐ

iti haṭha-pradīpikāyāṃ tṛtīyopadeśaḥ

End of chapter III, on the Exposition of the Mudrâs.

Chapter 4

Samadhi

Chaturthopadeśah

1.) namaḥ śivāya ghurave nāda-bindu-kalātmane I nirañjana-padaṃ yāti nityaṃ tatra parāyaṇaḥ

Salutation to the Gurû, the dispenser of happiness to all, appearing as Nâda, Vindû and Kalâ. One who is devoted to Him, obtains the highest bliss.

2.) athedānīṃ pravakṣhyāmi samādhikramamuttamam I mṝtyughnaṃ cha sukhopāyaṃ brahmānanda-karaṃ param

Now I will describe a regular method of attaining to Samâdhi, which destroys death, is the means for obtaining happiness, and gives the Brahmânanda.

3+4.) rāja-yoghaḥ samādhiścha unmanī cha manonmanī I amaratvaṃ layastattvaṃ śūnyāśūnyaṃ paraṃ padam

amanaskaṃ tathādvaitaṃ nirālambaṃ nirañjanam I jīvanmuktiścha sahajā turyā chetyeka-vāchakāḥ

Raja Yogî, Samâdhi, Unmani, Mauonmanî, Amarativa, Laya, Tatwa, Sûnya, Aśûnya, Parama Pada, Amanaska, Adwaitama, Nirãlamba, Nirañjana, Jîwana Mukti, Sahajâ, Turyâ, are all synonymous.

5.) salile saindhavaṃ yadvatsāmyaṃ bhajati yoghataḥ I tathātma-manasoraikyaṃ samādhirabhidhīyate

As salt being dissolved in water becomes one with it, so when Âtmâ and mind become one, it is called Samâdhi.

6.) yadā saṃkṣhīyate prāṇo mānasaṃ cha pralīyate I tadā samarasatvaṃ cha samādhirabhidhīyate

When the Prâna becomes lean (vigourless) and the mind becomes absorbed, then their becoming equal is called Samâdhi.

7.) tat-samaṃ cha dvayoraikyaṃ jīvātma-paramātmanoḥ I pranaṣhṭa-sarva-sangkalpaḥ samādhiḥ so|abhidhīyate

This equality and oneness of the self and the ultra self, when all Sankalpas cease to exist, is called Samâdhi.

8.) rāja-yoghasya māhātmyaṃ ko vā jānāti tattvataḥ I jñānaṃ muktiḥ sthitiḥ siddhirghu-ru-vākyena labhyate

Or, who can know the true greatness of the Raja Yoga. Knowledge, mukti, condition, and Siddhîs can be learnt by instructions from a gurû alone.

9.) durlabho viṣhaya-tyāgho durlabhaṃ tattva-darśanam I durlabhā sahajāvasthā sad-ghuroḥ karuṇāṃ vinā

Indifference to worldly enjoyments is very difficult to obtain, and equally difficult is the knowledge of the Realities to obtain. It is very difficult to get the condition of Samâdhi, without the favour of a true guru.

10.) vividhairāsanaiḥ kubhairvichitraiḥ ka-raṇairapi I prabuddhāyāṃ mahā-śaktau prāṇaḥ śūnye pralīyate

By means of various postures and different Kumbha-kas, when the great power (Kundalî) awakens, then the Prâna becomes absorbed in Sûnya (Samâdhi).

11.) utpanna-śakti-bodhasya tyak-ta-niḥśeṣha-karmaṇaḥ I yoghinaḥ sa-hajāvasthā svayameva prajāyate

The Yogî whose śakti has awakened, and who has renounced all actions, attains to the condition of Samâdhi, without any effort.

12.) suṣhumṇā-vāhini prāṇe śūnye viśati mānase I tadā sarvāṇi karmāṇi nirmūlayati yoghavit

When the Prâna flows in the Susumnâ, and the mind has entered śûnya, then the Yogî is free from the effects of Karmas.

13.) amarāya namastubhyaṃ so|api kālast-vayā jitaḥ I patitaṃ vadane yasya jaghade-tachcharācharam

O Immortal one (that is, the yogi who has attained to the condition of Samâdhi), I salute thee! Even death itself, into whose mouth the whole of this movable and immovable world has fallen, has been conquered by thee.

14.) chitte samatvamāpanne vāyau vraja-ti madhyame I tadāmarolī vajrolī sahajolī prajāyate

Amarolî, Vajrolî and Sahajolî are accomplished when

the mind becomes calm and Prâna has entered the middle channel.

15.) jñānaṃ kuto manasi sambhavatīha tāvat prāṇo|api jīvati mano mriyate na yāvat I prāṇo mano dvayamidaṃ vilayaṃ nayedyo mokṣhaṃ sa ghachchati naro na kathaṃchi-danyaḥ

How can it he possible to get knowledge, so long as the Prâna is living and the mind has not died? No one else can get moksa, except one who can make one's Prâna and mind latent.

16.) jñātvā suṣhumṇāsad-bhedaṃ kṛtvā vāyuṃ cha madhyagham I sthitvā sadaiva susthāne brahma-randhre nirodhayet

Always living in a good locality and having known the secret of the Susumnâ, which has a middle course, and making the Vâyu move in it., (the Yogî) should restrain the Vâyu in the Brahma randhra.

17.) sūrya-chandramasau dhattaḥ kālaṃ rātrindivātmakam I bhoktrī suṣhumnā kālasya ghuhyametadudāhṛtam

Time, in the form of night and day, is made by the sun and the moon. That, the Susumnâ devours this time (death) even, is a great secret.

18.) dvā-saptati-sahasrāṇi nāḍī-dvārāṇi pañjare I suṣhumṇā śāmbhavī śaktiḥ śeṣhāstveva nirarthakāḥ

In this body there are 72,000 openings of Nâdis; of these, the Susumnâ, which has the Śâmhhavî Sakti in it, is the only important one, the rest are useless.

19.) vāyuḥ parichito yasmādaghninā saha kuṇḍalīm I bodhayitvā suṣhumṇāyāṃ praviśedanirodhataḥ

The Vâyu should be made to enter the Susumnâ without restraint by him who has practised the control of breathing and has awakened the Kundali by the (gastric) fire.

20.) suṣhumṇā-vāhini prāṇe siddhyatyeva manonmanī I anyathā tvitarābhyāsāḥ prayāsāyaiva yoghinām

The Prâna, flowing through the Susumnâ, brings about the condition of manonmanî; other practices are simply futile for the Yogî.

21.) pavano badhyate yena manastenaiva badhyate I manaścha badhyate yena pavanastena badhyate

By whom the breathing has been controlled, by him the activities of the mind also have been controlled; and, conversely, by whom the activities of the mind have been controlled, by him the breathing also has been controlled.

22.) hetu-dvayaṃ tu chittasya vāsanā cha samīraṇaḥ I tayorvinaṣhṭa ekasmintau dvāvapi vinaśyataḥ

There are two causes of the activities of the mind: (1) Vâsanâ (desires) and (2) the respiration (the Prâna). Of these, the destruction of the one is the destruction of both.

23.) mano yatra vilīyeta pavanastatra līyate I pavano līyate yatra manastatra vilīyate

Breathing is lessened when the mind becomes absorbed, and the mind becomes absorbed when the Prâna is restrained.

24.) dughdhāmbuvatsaṃmilitāvubhau tau tulya-kriyau mānasa-mārutau hi I yato maruttatra manaḥ-pravṝttir yato manastatra marut-pravṝttiḥ

Both the mind and the breath are united together, like milk and water; and both of them are equal in their activities. Mind begins its activities where there is the breath, and the Parana begins its activities where there is the mind.

25.) atraika-nāśādaparasya nāśa eka-pravṝt-terapara-pravṝttiḥ I adhvastayośchend-riya-vargha-vṝttiḥ pradhvastayormokṣha-pa-dasya siddhiḥ

By the suspension of the one, therefore, comes the suspension of the other, and by the operations of the one are brought about the operations of the other. When they are present, the Indriyas (the senses) remain en-gaged in their proper functions, and when they become latent then there is moksa.

26.) rasasya manasaśchaiva chañchalatvaṃ svabhāvataḥ I raso baddho mano baddhaṃ kiṃ na siddhyati bhūtale

By nature, Mercury and mind are unsteady: there is nothing in the world which cannot be accomplished when these are made steady.

27.) mūrchchito harate vyādhīnmṝto jīvayati svayam I baddhaḥ khecharatāṃ dhatte raso vāyuścha pārvati

O Pârvati! Mercury and breathing, when made steady, destroy diseases and the dead himself comes to life (by their means). By their (proper) control, moving in the air is attained.

28.) manaḥ sthairyaṃ sthiro vāyustato binduḥ sthiro bhavet I bindu-sthairyātsadā sattvaṃ piṇḍa-sthairyaṃ prajāyate

The breathing is calmed when the mind becomes steady and calm; and hence the preservation of bindu. The preservation of this latter makes the satwa established in the body.

29.) indriyāṇāṃ mano nātho manonāthastu mārutaḥ I mārutasya layo nāthaḥ sa layo nādamāśritaḥ

Mind is the master of the senses, and the breath is the

master of the mind. The breath in its turn is subordinate to the laya (absorption), and that laya depends on the nâda.

30.) so|ayamevāstu mokṣhākhyo māstu vāpi matāntare I manaḥ-prāṇa-laye kaśchidānandaḥ sampravartate

This very laya is what is called moksa, or, being a sectarian, you may not call it moksa; but when the mind becomes absorbed, a sort of ecstacy is experienced.

31.) pranaṣhṭa-śvāsa-niśvāsaḥ pradhvasta-viṣhaya-ghrahaḥ I niścheṣhṭo nirvikāraścha layo jayati yoghinām

By the suspension of respiration and the annihilation of the enjoyments of the senses, when the mind becomes devoid of all the activities and remains changeless, then the Yogî attains to the Laya Stage.

32.) uchchinna-sarva-sangkalp-niḥśeṣhāśeṣha-cheṣhṭitaḥ I svāvaghamyo layaḥ ko|api jāyate vāgh-aghocharaḥ

All the prominent desires being entirely finished, and the body motionless, results in the absorption or laya, which is only known by the Self, and beyond the scope of words.

33.) yatra dṝṣhṭirlayastatra bhūtend-riya-sanātanī I sā śaktirjīva-bhūtānāṃ dve alakṣhye layaṃ ghate

Where the sight is directed, absorption occurs. That in which the elements, senses and shakti exist externally, which is in all living things, both ore dissolved in the characteristicless.

34.) layo laya iti prāhuḥ kīdṝśaṃ laya-lakṣhaṇam I apunar-vāsanotthānāllayo viṣhaya-vismṝtiḥ

Some say 'laya, laya' but what is the characteristic of laya or absorption? Laya is the non-recollection of the objects of the senses when the previous deep-rooted desires (and impressions) are non-recurrent.

35.) veda-śāstra-purāṇāni sāmānya-ghaṇikā iva I ekaiva śāmbhavī mudrā ghuptā ku-la-vadhūriva

The Vedas, shastras and Puranas are like common women, but shambhavi is secret like a woman of good heritage.

36.) atha śāmbhavī

antarlakṣhyaṃ bahirdṝṣhṭirnimeṣhonme-ṣha-varjitā I eṣhā sā śāmbhavī mudrā ve-da-śāstreṣhu ghopitā

The Sâmbhavî Mudrâ.

With internalized (one-pointed) awareness and external gaze unblinking, that verily is shambhavi mudra, pre-served in the Vedas.

37.) antarlakṣhya-vilīna-chitta-pavano yoghī yadā vartate dṝṣhṭyā niśchala-tārayā bahirad-haḥ paśyannapaśyannapi I mudreyaṃ khalu śāmbhavī bhavati sā labdhā prasādādghuroḥ śūnyāśūnya-vilakṣhaṇaṃ sphurati tattattvaṃ padaṃ śāmbhavam

When the Yogî remains inwardly attentive to the Brah-man, keeping the mind and the Prâna absorbed, and the sight steady, as if seeing everything while in reality seeing nothing outside, below, or above, verily then it is called the Sâmbhavî Mudrâ, which is learnt by the fa-vour of a guru. Whatever, wonderful, Sûnya or Asûnya is perceived, is to be regarded as the manifestation of that great Śambhû (Śiva.)

38.) śrī-śāmbhavyāścha khecharyā avast-hā-dhāma-bhedataḥ I bhavechchitta-layā-nandaḥ śūnye chit-sukha-rūpiṇi

The two states, the Sâmbhavî and the Khecharî, are different because of their seats (being the heart and the space between the eyebrows respectively); but both cause happiness, for the mind becomes absorbed in the Chita-sukha-Rupa-âtmana which is void.

39.) tāre jyotiṣhi saṃyojya kiṃchidunnamay-edbhruvau I pūrva-yoghaṃ mano yuñjan-nunmanī-kārakaḥ kṣhaṇāt

With perfect concentration, the pupils fixed on the light by raising the eyebrows up a little, as from the previously described (shambhavi), mind is joined and instantly unmani occurs.

40.) kechidāghama-jālena kechinnigha-ma-sangkulaiḥ I kechittarkeṇa muhyanti naiva jānanti tārakam

Some are devoted to the Vedas, some to Nigama, while others are enwrapt in Logic, but none knows the value of this mudrâ, which enables one to cross the ocean of existence.

41.) ardhonmīlita-lochanaḥ sthira-manā nāsāghra-dattekṣhaṇaś chandrārkāvapi līnatāmupanayannispanda-bhāvena yaḥ I jyotī-rūpamaśeṣha-bījamakhilaṃ dedīpyamānaṃ paraṃ tattvaṃ tat-padameti vastu paramaṃ vāchyaṃ kimatrādhikam

With steady calm mind and half closed eyes, fixed on the tip of the nose, stopping the Idâ and the Pingalâ without blinking, he who can see the light which is the all, the seed, the entire brilliant, great Tatwama, approaches Him, who is the great object. What is the use of more talk?

42.) divā na pūjayellinggghaṃ rātrau chaiva na pūjayet I sarvadā pūjayellinggghaṃ divārātri-nirodhataḥ

One should not meditate on the Linga (i.e., Âtman) in the day (i.e., while Sûrya or Pingalâ is working) or at night (when Idâ is working), but should always contemplate after restraining both.

43.) atha khecharī savya-dakṣhiṇa-nāḍī-stho madhye charati mārutaḥ I tiṣhṭhate khecharī mudrā tasminsthāne na saṃśayaḥ

The Khecharî.

When the prana which is in the right and left nadis moves m the middle nadi (sushumna) that is the condition for khechari mudra.

44.) iḍā-pingghalayormadhye śūnyaṃ chaivānilaṃ ghraset I tiṣhṭhate khecharī mudrā tatra satyaṃ punaḥ punaḥ

The fire (of shakti) being swallowed (suppressed) midway between, ida and pingala, in that shoonya (of sushumna), is in truth the condition for khechari mudra.

45.) sūrchyāchandramasormadhye nirālambāntare punaḥ I saṃsthitā vyoma-chakre yā sā mudrā nāma khecharī

That Mudrâ is called Khecharî which is performed in the supportless space between the Sûrya and the Chandra (the Idâ and the Pingalâ) and called the Vyoma Chakra.

46.) somādyatroditā dhārā sākṣhātsā śiva-vallabhā I pūrayedatulāṃ divyāṃ suṣhumṇāṃ paśchime mukhe

The Khecharî which causes the stream to flow from the Chandra (Śoma) is beloved of Śiva. The incomparable divine Susumnâ should be closed by the tongue drawn back.

47.) purastāchchaiva pūryeta niśchitā khecharī bhavet I abhyastā khecharī mudrāpyunmanī samprajāyate

It can be closed from the front also (by stopping the movements of the Prâna), and then surely it becomes the Khecharî. By practice, this Khecharî leads to Unmanî.

48.) bhruvormadhye śiva-sthānaṃ manastatra vilīyate I jñātavyaṃ tat-padaṃ turyaṃ tatra kālo na vidyate

In the middle of the Eyebrows is the place of Shiva, there the mind is quiescent. That state is known as turiya or the fourth dimension. There, time is unknown.

49.) abhyasetkhecharīṃ tāvadyāvatsyādyogha-nidritaḥ I samprāpta-yogha-nidrasya kālo nāsti kadāchana

The Khecharî should be practised till there is Yoga-nidrâ (Samâdhi). One who has induced Yoga-nidrâ, cannot fall a victim to death.

50.) nirālambaṃ manaḥ kṝtvā na kiṃchida-pi chintayet I sa-bāhyābhyantaraṃ vyomni ghaṭavattiṣhṭhati dhruvam

Freeing the mind from all thoughts and thinking of nothing, one should sit firmly like a pot in the space (surrounded and filled with the ether).

51.) bāhya-vāyuryathā līnastathā madhyo na saṃśayaḥ I sva-sthāne sthiratāmeti pavano manasā saha

As the air, in and out of the body, remains unmoved, so the breath with mind becomes steady in its place (i.e., in Brahma randhra).

52.) evamabhyasyatastasya vāyu-mārghe divāniśam I abhyāsājjīryate vāyurmanasta-traiva līyate

By thus practising, night and day, the breathing is brought under control, and, as the practice increases, the mind becomes calm and steady.

53.) amṝtaiḥ plāvayeddehamāpāda-tala-mas-takam I siddhyatyeva mahā-kāyo mahā-ba-la-parākramaḥ

By rubbing the body over with Amrita (exuding from the moon), from head to foot, one gets Mahâkâyâ, i.e., great strength and energy.

End of the Khecharî.

54.) śakti-madhye manaḥ kṝtvā śaktiṃ mā-nasa-madhyaghām I manasā mana ālokya dhārayetparamaṃ padam

Placing the mind into the Kundalini, and getting the latter into the mind, by looking upon the Buddhi (intellect) with mind (reflexively), the Param Pada (Brahma) should be obtained.

55.) kha-madhye kuru chātmānamātma-madhye cha khaṃ kuru I sarvaṃ cha kha-mayaṃ kṝtvā na kiṃchidapi chintayet

Keep the âtmâ inside the Kha (Brahma) and place Brahma inside your âtmâ. Having made everything pervaded with Kha (Brahma), think of nothing else.

56.) antaḥ śūnyo bahiḥ śūnyaḥ śūnyaḥ kum-bha ivāmbare I antaḥ pūrṇo bahiḥ pūrṇaḥ pūrṇaḥ kumbha ivārṇave

One should become void in and void out, and voice like a pot in the space. Full in and full outside, like a jar in the ocean.

57.) bāhya-chintā na kartavyā tathaivāntara-chintanam I sarva-chintāṃ parityajya na kiṃchidapi chintayet

He should be neither of his inside nor of outside world; and, leaving all thoughts, he should think of nothing.

58.) sangkalpa-mātra-kalanaiva jaghatsamaghraṃ sangkalpa-mātra-kalanaiva mano-vilāsaḥ I sangkalpa-mātra-matimutsṛja nirvikalpam āśritya niśchayamavāpnuhi rāma śāntim

The whole of this world and all the schemes of the mind are but the creations of thought. Discarding these thoughts and taking leave of all conjectures, O Râma! obtain peace.

59.) karpūramanale yadvatsaindhavaṃ salile yathā I tathā sandhīyamānaṃ cha manastattve vilīyate

As camphor disappears in fire, and rock salt in water, so the mind united with the âtmâ loses its identity.

60.) jñeyaṃ sarvaṃ pratītaṃ cha jñānaṃ cha mana uchyate I jñānaṃ jñeyaṃ samaṃ naṣhṭaṃ nānyaḥ panthā dvitīyakaḥ

When the knowable, and the knowledge, are both destroyed equally, then there is no second way (i.e., Duality is destroyed).

61.) mano-dṛśyamidaṃ sarvaṃ yat-kiṃchitsa-charācharam I manaso hyun-manī-bhāvāddvaitaṃ naivolabhyate

All this movable and immovable world is mind. When the mind has attained to the unmanî avasthâ, there is no dwaita (from the absence of the working of the mind.)

62.) jñeya-vastu-parityāghādvilayaṃ yāti mānasam I manaso vilaye jāte kaivalyama-vaśiṣhyate

Mind disappears by removing the knowable, and, on its disappearance, âtmâ only remains behind.

63.) evaṃ nānā-vidhopāyāḥ samy-aksvānubhavānvitāḥ I samādhi-mārghāḥ kathitāḥ pūrvāchāryairmahātmabhiḥ

The high-souled Âchâryas (Teachers) of yore gained experience in the various methods of Samâdhi themselves, and then they preached them to others.

64.) suṣhumṇāyai kuṇḍalinyai sudhāyai chandra-janmane I manonmanyai namastubhyaṃ mahā-śaktyai chid-ātmane

Salutations to Thee, O Susumnâ, to Thee O Kundalinî, to Thee O Sudhâ, born of Chandra, to Thee O Manomnanî! to Thee O great power, energy and the intelligent spirit.

65.) aśakya-tattva-bodhānāṃ mūḍhānāmapi saṃmatam I proktaṃ ghorakṣha-nāthena nādopāsanamuchyate

I will describe now the practice of anâhata nâda, as propounded by Goraksa Nâtha, for the benefit of those who are unable to understand the principles of knowledge—a method, which is liked by the ignorant also.

66.) śrī-ādināthena sa-pāda-koṭi-laya-prakārāḥ kathitā jayanti I nādānusandhānakamekameva manyāmahe mukhyatamaṃ layānām

Âdinâtha propounded 1¼ crore methods of trance, and

they are all extant. Of these, the hearing of the anâhata nâda is the Only one, the chief, in my opinion.

67.) muktāsane sthito yoghī mudrāṃ sandhāya śāmbhavīm I śṝṇuyāddakṣhiṇe karṇe nādamantāsthamekadhīḥ

Sitting with Mukta Âsana and with the Sâmbhavî Madill, the Yogî should hear the sound inside his right ear, with collected mind.

68.) śravaṇa-puṭa-nayana-yughala ghrāṇa-mukhānāṃ nirodhanaṃ kāryam I śuddha-suṣhumṇā-saraṇau sphuṭamamalaḥ śrūyate nādaḥ

The ears, the eyes, the nose, and the mouth should be closed and then the clear sound is heard in the passage of the Susumnâ which has been cleansed of all its impurities.

69.) ārambhaścha ghaṭaśchaiva tathā parichayo|api cha I niṣhpattiḥ sarva-yogheṣhu syādavasthā-chatuṣhṭayam

In all the Yogas, there are four states: (1) ârambha or the preliminary, (2) Ghata, or the state of a jar, (3) Parichaya (known), (4) nispatti (consumate.)

70.) atha ārambhāvasthā
brahma-ghrantherbhavedbhedo hyānandaḥ śūnya-sambhavaḥ I vichitraḥ kvaṇako de-he|anāhataḥ śrūyate dhvaniḥ

Ârambha Avasthâ.

When the Brahma granthi (in the heart) is pierced through by Prânâyâma, then a sort of happiness is experienced in the vacuum of the heart, and the anâhat sounds, like various tinkling sounds of ornaments, are heard in the body.

71.) divya-dehaścha tejasvī divya-ghandhas-tvaroghavān I sampūrṇa-hṝdayaḥ śūnya ārambhe yoghavānbhavet

In the ârambha, a Yogî's body becomes divine, glowing, healthy, and emits a divine swell. The whole of his heart becomes void.

72.) atha ghaṭāvasthā
dvitīyāyāṃ ghaṭīkṝtya vāyurbhavati mad-hyaghaḥ I dṝḍhāsano bhavedyoghī jñānī deva-samastadā

The Ghata Avasthâ.

In the second stage, the airs are united into one and begin moving in the middle channel. The Yogî's posture becomes firm, and he becomes wise like a god.

73.) viṣhṇu-ghranthestato bhedātparamā-nanda-sūchakaḥ I atiśūnye vimardaścha bherī-śabdastadā bhavet

By this means the Vishu knot (in the throat) is pierced which is indicated by highest pleasure experienced, And then the Bherî sound (like the beating of a kettle drain) is evolved in the vacuum in the throat.

74.) atha parichayāvasthā tṛtīyāyāṃ tu vijñeyo vihāyo mardala-dhva-niḥ I mahā-śūnyaṃ tadā yāti sarva-sidd-hi-samāśrayam

The Parichaya Avasthâ.

In the third stage, the sound of a drum is known to arise in tie Sûnya between the eyebrows, and then the Vâyu goes to the Mahâśûnya, which is the home of all the siddhîs.

75.) chittānandaṃ tadā jitvā sahajānanda-sambhavaḥ I doṣha-duḥkha-jarā-vyādhi-kṣhudhā-nidrā-vivarjitaḥ

Conquering, then, the pleasures of the mind, ecstacy is spontaneously produced which is devoid of evils, pains, old age, disease, hunger and sleep.

76.) atha niṣhpatty-avasthā rudra-ghranthiṃ yadā bhittvā śarva-pīṭha-ghato|anilaḥ | niṣhpattau vaiṇavaḥ śabdaḥ kvaṇad-vīṇā-kvaṇo bhavet

The Nishpatty Avasthâ.

When the Rudra granthi is pierced and the air enters the seat of the Lord (the space between the eyebrows), then the perfect sound like that of a flute is produced.

77.) ekībhūtaṃ tadā chittaṃ rāja-yoghābhidhānakam I sṛṣhṭi-saṃhāra-kartāsau yoghīśvara-samo bhavet

The union of the mind and the sound is called the Râja-Yoga. The (real) Yogî becomes the creator and destroyer of the universe, like God.

78.) astu vā māstu vā muktiratraivākhaṇḍi-taṃ sukham I layodbhavamidaṃ saukhyaṃ rāja-yoghādavāpyate

Perpetual Happiness is achieved by this; I do not care if the mukti be not attained. This happiness, resulting from absorption [in Brahma], is obtained by means of Raja-Yoga.

79.) rāja-yoghamajānantaḥ kevalaṃ haṭha-karmiṇaḥ I etānabhyāsino manye prayāsa-phala-varjitān

Those who are ignorant of the Râja-Yoga and practise only the Hatha-Yoga, will, in my opinion, waste their energy fruitlessly.

80.) unmany-avāptaye śīghraṃ bhrū-dhyā-naṃ mama saṃmatam I rāja-yogha-padaṃ prāptuṃ sukhopāyo|alpa-chetasām I sadyaḥ pratyaya-sandhāyī jāyate nādajo layaḥ

Contemplation on the space between the eyebrows is, in my opinion, best for accomplishing soon the Unmanî state. For people of small intellect, it is a very easy method for obtaining perfection in the Raja-Yoga. The Laya produced by nâda, at once gives experience (of spiritual powers).

81.) nādānusandhāna-samādhi-bhājāṃ yoghīśvarāṇāṃ hṝdi vardhamānam I ānandamekaṃ vachasāmaghamyaṃ jānāti taṃ śrī-ghurunātha ekaḥ

The happiness which increases in the hearts of Yogiśwaras, who have gained success in Samâdhi by means of attention to the nâda, is beyond description, and is known to Śri Gurû Nâtha alone.

82.) karṇau pidhāya hastābhyāṃ yaḥ śṝṇoti dhvaniṃ muniḥ I tatra chittaṃ sthirīkuryādyāvatsthira-padaṃ vrajet

The sound which a muni hears by closing his ears with his fingers, should be heard attentively, till the mind becomes steady in it.

83.) abhyasyamāno nādo|ayaṃ bāhyamāvṝṇute dhvanim I pakṣhādvikṣhepamakhilaṃ jitvā yoghī sukhī bhavet

By practising with this nâda, all other external sounds are stopped. The Yogî becomes happy by overcoming all distractions within 15 days.

84.) śrūyate prathamābhyāse nādo nānā-vidho mahān I tato|abhyāse vardhamāne śrūyate sūkṣhma-sūkṣhmakaḥ

In the beginning, the sounds heard are of great variety and very loud; but, as the practice increases, they become more and more subtle.

85.) ādau jaladhi-jīmūta-bherī-jharjhara-sambhavāḥ I madhye mardala-śangkhotthā ghaṇṭā-kāhalajāstathā

In the first stage, the sounds are surging, thundering like the beating of kettle drums and jingling ones. In the intermediate stage, they are like those produced by conch, Mridanga, bells, &c.

86.) ante tu kingkiṇī-vaṃśa-vīṇā-bhramara-niḥsvanāḥ I iti nānāvidhā nādāḥ śrūyante deha-madhyaghāḥ

In the last stage, the sounds resemble those from tinklets, flute, bee, &c. These various kinds of sounds are heard as being produced in the body.

87.) mahati śrūyamāṇe|api megha-bhery-ādike dhvanau I tatra sūkṣhmātsūkṣhmataraṃ nādameva parāmṛśet

Though hearing loud sounds like those of thunder, kettle drums, etc. one should practise with the subtle sounds also.

88.) ghanamutsṝjya vā sūkṣhme sūkṣhmam-utsṝjya vā ghane I ramamāṇamapi kṣhiptaṃ mano nānyatra chālayet

Leaving the loudest, taking up the subtle one, and leaving the subtle one, taking up the loudest, thus practising, the distracted mind does not wander elsewhere.

89.) yatra kutrāpi vā nāde laghati prathamaṃ manaḥ I tatraiva susthirībhūya tena sārdhaṃ vilīyate

Wherever the mind attaches itself first, it becomes steady there; and then it becomes absorbed in it.

90.) makarandaṃ pibanbhṝngghī ghandhaṃ nāpekṣhate yathā I nādāsaktaṃ tathā chittaṃ viṣhayānnahi kāngkṣhate

Just as a bee, drinking sweet juice, does not care for the smell of the flower; so the mind, absorbed in the nâda, does not desire the objects of enjoyment.

91.) mano-matta-ghajendrasya viṣhayodyā-na-chāriṇaḥ I samartho|ayaṃ niyamane nināda-niśitāngkuśaḥ

The mind, like an elephant habituated to wander in the garden of enjoyments, is capable of being controlled by the sharp goad of anâhata nâda.

92.) baddhaṃ tu nāda-bandhena manaḥ san-tyakta-chāpalam I prayāti sutarāṃ sthairyaṃ chinna-pakṣhaḥ khagho yathā

The mind, captivated in the snare of nâda, gives up all its activity; and, like a bird with clipped wings, becomes calm at once.

93.) sarva-chintāṃ parityajya sāvadhānena chetasā I nāda evānusandheyo yogha-sām-rājyamichchatā

Those desirous of the kingdom of Yoga, should take up the practice of hearing the anâhata nâda, with mind collected and free from all cares.

94.) nādo|antaranggha-sāranggha-bandhane vāghurāyate I antaranggha-kurangghasya vadhe vyādhāyate|api cha

Nada is the snare for catching the mind; and, when it is caught like a deer, it can be killed also like it.

95.) antarangghasya yamino vājinaḥ parig-hāyate I nādopāsti-rato nityamavadhāryā hi yoghinā

Nâda is the bolt of the stable door for the horse (the minds of the Yogîs). A Yogî should determine to practise constantly in the hearing of the nâda sounds.

96.) baddhaṃ vimukta-chāñchalyaṃ nā-da-ghandhaka-jāraṇāt I manaḥ-pāradamāp-noti nirālambākhya-khe|aṭanam

Mind gets the properties of calcined mercury. When deprived of its unsteadiness it is calcined, combined with the sulphur of nâda, and then it roams like it in tine supportless âkâśa or Brahma. 95.

97.) nāda-śravaṇataḥ kṣhipramantarangg-ha-bhujangghamam I vismṟtaya sarva-mekāghraḥ kutrachinnahi dhāvati

The mind is like a serpent, forgetting all its unsteadiness by hearing the nâda, it does not run away anywhere.

98.) kāṣhṭhe pravartito vahniḥ kāṣhṭhena saha śāmyati I nāde pravartitaṃ chittaṃ nādena saha līyate

The fire, catching firewood, is extinguished along with it (after burning it up); and so the mind also, working with the nâda, becomes latent along with it.

99.) ghaṇṭādināda-sakta-stabdhāntaḥ-karaṇa-hariṇasya I praharaṇamapi sukaraṃ syāchchara-sandhāna-pravīṇaśchet

The antahkarana (mind), like a deer, becomes absorbed and motionless on hearing the sound of hells, etc. and then it is very easy for an expert archer to kill it.

100.) anāhatasya śabdasya dhvanirya upalabhyate I dhvanerantarghataṃ jñeyaṃ jñeyasyāntarghataṃ manaḥ I manastatra layaṃ yāti tadviṣhṇoḥ paramaṃ padam

The knowable interpenetrates the anâhata sound which is heard, and the mind interpenetrates the knowable. The mind becomes absorbed there, which is the seat of the all-pervading, almighty Lord.

101.) tāvadākāśa-sangkalpo yāvachchabdaḥ pravartate I niḥśabdaṃ tat-paraṃ brahma paramāteti ghīyate

So long as the sounds continue, there is the idea of âkâśa. When they disappear, then it is called Para Brahma, Paramâtmana.

102.) yatkiṃchinnāda-rūpeṇa śrūyate śaktireva sā I yastattvānto nirākāraḥ sa eva parameśvaraḥ

Whatever is heard in the form of nâda, is the śakti (power). That which is formless, the final state of the Tatwas, is tile Parameśwara.

103.) iti nādānusandhānam
sarve haṭha-layopāyā rājayoghasya siddhaye I rāja-yogha-samārūḍhaḥ puruṣhaḥ kāla-vañchakaḥ

All the methods of Hatha are meant for gaining success in the Raja-Yoga; for, the man, who is well-established in the Raja-Yoga, overcomes death.

104.) tattvaṃ bījaṃ haṭhaḥ kṣhetramaudāsīnyaṃ jalaṃ tribhiḥ I unmanī kalpa-latikā sadya eva pravartate

Tatwa is the seed, Hatha the field; and Indifference (Vairâgya) the water. By the action of these three, the creeper Unmanî thrives very rapidly.

105.) sadā nādānusandhānātkṣhīyante pāpa-saṃchayāḥ I nirañjane vilīyete niśchitaṃ chitta-mārutau

All the accumulations of sins are destroyed by practising always with the nâda; and the mind and the airs do certainly become latent in the colorless (Paramâtmana).

106.) śangkha-dundhubhi-nādaṃ cha na śṝṇoti kadāchana I kāṣhṭhavajjāyate deha unmanyāvasthayā dhruvam

Such a one. does not hear the noise of the conch and Dundubhi. Being in the Unmanî avasthâ, his body becomes like a piece of wood.

107.) sarvāvasthā-vinirmuktaḥ sarva-chintā-vivarjitaḥ I mṝtavattiṣhṭhate yoghī sa mukto nātra saṃśayaḥ

There is no doubt, such a Yogî becomes free from all states, from all cares, and remains like one dead.

108.) khādyate na cha kālena bādhyate na cha karmaṇā I sādhyate na sa kenāpi yoghī yuktaḥ samādhinā

He is not devoured by death, is not bound by his actions. The Yogî who is engaged in Samâdhi is over-powered by none.

109.) na ghandhaṃ na rasaṃ rūpaṃ na cha sparśaṃ na niḥsvanam I nātmānaṃ na paraṃ vetti yoghī yuktaḥ samādhinā

The Yogî, engaged in Samâdhi, feels neither smell, taste, color, touch, sound, nor is conscious of his own self.

110.) chittaṃ na suptaṃ nojāghratsmṝti-vismṝti-varjitam I na chāstameti nodeti yasyāsau mukta eva saḥ

He whose mind is neither sleeping, waking, remembering, destitute of memory, disappearing nor appearing, is liberated.

111.) na vijānāti śītoṣhṇaṃ na duḥkhaṃ na sukhaṃ tathā I na mānaṃ nopamānaṃ cha yoghī yuktaḥ samādhinā

He feels neither heat, cold, pain, pleasure, respect nor disrespect. Such a Yogî is absorbed in Samâdhi.

112.) svastho jāghradavasthāyāṃ suptava-dyo|avatiṣhṭhate I niḥśvāsochchvāsa-hī-naścha niśchitaṃ mukta eva saḥ

He who, though awake, appears like one sleeping, and is without inspiration and expiration, is certainly free.

113.) avadhyaḥ sarva-śastrāṇāmaśakyaḥ sar-va-dehinām I aghrāhyo mantra-yantrāṇāṃ yoghī yuktaḥ samādhinā

The Yogî, engaged in Samâdhi, cannot be killed by any instrument, and is beyond the controlling power of bein-gs. He is beyond the reach of incantations and charms.

114.) yāvadvidurna bhavati dṛḍhaḥ prāṇa-vā-ta-prabandhāt I yāvaddhyāne saha-ja-sadṛśaṃ jāyate naiva tattvaṃ tāvajjñānaṃ vadati tadidaṃ dambha-mithyā-pralāpaḥ

As long as the Prâna does not enter and flow in the middle channel and the vindu does not become firm by the control of the movements of the Prâna; as long as the mind does not assume the form of Brahma without any effort in contemplation, so long all the talk of knowledge and wisdom is merely the nonsensical babbling of a mad man.

ॐ

iti haṭha-yogha-pradīpikāyāṃ samād-hi-lakṣhaṇaṃ nāma chaturthopadeśaḥ |

THE END.